SOUTH AFRICA UNDER MAJORITY RULE

SOUTH AFRICA UNDER MAJORITY RULE
A Study in Power Sharing,
Racial Equality and Democracy

Thomas K. Ranuga

African Studies
Volume 54

The Edwin Mellen Press
Lewiston•Queenston•Lampeter

Library of Congress Cataloging-in-Publication Data

Ranuga, Thomas K., 1938-
   South Africa under majority rule : a study in power sharing, racial equality and democracy / Thomas K. Ranuga.
     p. cm. -- (African studies ; v. 54)
   Includes index.
   ISBN 0-7734-7716-0
    1. Democracy--South Africa. 2. Race relations. 3. Ethnic relations--South Africa--Political aspects. 4. South Africa--Race relations. 5. South Africa--Ethnic relations--Political aspects. 6. South Africa--Politics and government--1994- I. Title. II. African studies (Lewiston, N.Y.) ; v. 54.

JQ1981 .R36 2000
968.06'5--dc21

                                                           00-032450

This is volume 54 in the continuing series
African Studies
Volume 54 ISBN 0-7734-7716-0
AS Series ISBN 0-88946-175-9

A CIP catalog record for this book is available from the British Library.

The Edwin Mellen Press   The Edwin Mellen Press
Box 450   Box 67
Lewiston, New York   Queenston, Ontario
USA 14092-0450   CANADA L0S 1L0

The Edwin Mellen Press, Ltd.
Lampeter, Ceredigion, Wales
UNITED KINGDOM SA48 8LT

Printed in the United States of America

To my wife Thembi and sons Mpumi, Dumi, and Siso

CONTENTS

PART I
RESPONSES TO STRUCTURED QUESTIONS   13

LIST OF TABLES

Table

Preface

The great historical experiment called South Africa embarked upon another of its phases when it held its first all-race elections in 1994. The country was subjugated to European rule, first by the Dutch beginning in 1652, and then by the British, leading eventually to the apartheid system put in place in 1948 by the Nationalist Party of Afrikaners. Of course the intervening three centuries were marked by resistance, conflict and violence between the white and non-white groups. The apartheid system was one of the most insidious systems of social and political control ever devised, but its greatest shock value is the fact that it emerged fully only in the last half of the 20th century. The 1994 elections were the first time in south Africa's history that non-whites could vote and thus mark a great reversal of a long-standing political and social evil.

It is all the most remarkable, therefore, given the system of apartheid with every form of discrimination and inequality put to use, that South Africa could produce the leaders who would save the country from civil war and the attendant suffering that would ensue-- physical, psychological, and economic. As the author of this report informs us, South Africans, and especially South Africa university students, gratefully acknowledge the leadership roles played by F. de Klerk and Nelson Mandela in pulling the country back from the abyss.

But with the establishment in 1994 of the Government of National Unity (GNU), the holding of the nation's first non-racial elections, and the imposition of a new constitutional order, a whole new range of questions loom ahead. Will the new South African elite, drawn from the universities, continue on the path of power sharing, reconciliation, and rapprochement? Or will the exigencies of economic want, the need for radical economic re-structuring, educational reform, and even psychological retribution gain the upper hand and lead to Black domination and perhaps a reverse form of discrimination to compensate for the wounds of the past?

Professor Thomas Ranuga's timely study gives us many new insights into these questions, along with considerable reason for optimism. Recognizing that South Africa's future depends on its emerging elite and that these will be drawn largely from the country's universities, Professor Ranuga in 1995 set about interviewing students all over the country to find answers to questions about the role of democracy and power sharing, economic and ethnic equality, the role of political parties, and not least of all, the perceptions of the effectiveness of affirmative action should that expedient be deemed necessary in the remaking of South Africa.

Undoubtedly one of the most striking findings of this study is the fact that the majority of South African university students -- Black, Colored, Indian, White and Afrikaner-- all agree that some form of power sharing is necessary, at least for the present. A strictly democratic alternative based on majority rule suggests to most respondents the emergence of Black domination, something that most South Africans do not seem to want. That <u>Black</u> South Africans should hold this view, and not wish to simply reverse the tables and dominate their non-Black compatriots after so many years of white oppression, seems to this reader a marvel of history and a very good omen for the future. Readers of this book may want to consider it a precise clinical snapshot taken along the path of a momentous historical journey. It provides a very rich diet of opinion systematically drawn from the ranks of the future elite of South Africa. It also stands as a landmark against which to evaluate future developments.

Toby E. Huff
Chancellor Professor
Department of Sociology & Anthropology, UMass Darthmouth .

vi

ACKNOWLEDGMENTS

It was in 1994, after the historic elections that marked the birth of the new South Africa, that I decided to apply for a 1995 sabbatical leave from the University of Massachusetts Dartmouth, where I was a Professor of Sociology. I wanted to undertake a research project that would focus on the attitudes of South African university students to the concepts of power sharing, racial equality, democracy and other related matters. From the beginning to the end, I received inspiration and tangible support from a number of individuals who played important roles at various stages of my work. I am deeply grateful to all these individuals to whom I owe an intellectual debt of acknowledgment. I extend my sincere thanks to every one of them.

The initial research design of the project was intensively analyzed and methodically reviewed by a number of my professional colleagues at the University of Massachusetts Dartmouth whose constructive perspectives were very helpful, particularly in the area of theoretical conceptualization and methodology. These include Professor Toby E. Huff in my Department of Sociology/Anthropology, Professor Morton H. Elfenbein of the Psychology Department, and Professors John J. Carroll and Shaukat Ali of the Political Science Department. Carroll McCloud, the Director of Frederick Douglass Unity House, read the manuscript and made constructive and helpful suggestions.

The photograph for the front cover was taken by Deirdre Confar of Photographics under the supervision of Professor Ziddi Msangi of the College of Visual and Performing Arts. Peggy Dias took the photo portrait for the back cover. Richard Legault II made a substantial contribution with his computer skills. My profound thanks to all these individuals for their time and expertise.

At the University of the North in South Africa, where I was based for my sabbatical research, I received strong support from Professor S. Motshologane who saw to it personally, as the Dean of Arts, that I received all the institutional support I needed to carry out my work. And, at my service all the time, even above and beyond the call of duty, was the indefatigable Dennis Nhlanhla Nkosi, a lecturer in the Department of Sociology. My research assistant, Ms. Nigist Bekele, did an excellent job as a computer analyst and compiler of research data.

The questionnaire used in the survey was already constructed before my departure for South Africa but, upon arrival there, it received further scrutiny from Ms. Elirea Bornman, a researcher at the Human Science Research Council in Pretoria (now with a D.Litt. et Phil. degree), who made very constructive suggestions and asked to append five questions relating to culture and ethnicity that she wanted to use for her own research. Ms. Bornman was also of immense help in enlisting the services of Professor Johannes Bernardus Schoeman who organized the distribution of the questionnaire to students at the University of Pretoria.

Since my research involved nine universities scattered in different parts of the country, it would have been very difficult for me to supervise the distribution of the questionnaire and collect the responses, were it not for the admirable support I received from the individuals located at those universities.

Mxolisi Mgxashe, a true and trusted friend, organized contact persons at the three universities in the Western Cape: Professor Itumeleng J. Mosala, Dr. Nosiza Matshiliza and Dr. Moses Mbeo at the University of Cape Town; Professor Kwesi Prah at the University of the Western Cape; and Mhlobo Jadezweni at the University of Stellenbosch. In the course of my visits to these three universities, Ms. Imelda Whittaker provided necessary transportation and friendly company.

At other universities, the following individuals contributed their invaluable services in organizing the distribution and collection of the questionnaire:

Professor Mbulelo Mzamane and Mr. Nico Jooste at the University of Fort Hare;

Ms. Peggy Msimango at the University of Durban-Westville;

Mr. Bheki Peterson at the University of the Witwatersrand;

and Mr. Godffrey Tshabalala at the University of Zululand.

Special mention must be made of an old friend of mine from primary school days through secondary and post secondary education, Rev. Lebamang J. Sebidi, my main contact person in South Africa. He has always been very generous with his time and genuine brotherly support and was very helpful in collecting missing statistical information for me. He also introduced me to Mr. Chris van Wyk who offered his services to locate a suitable publisher in South Africa. I am immensely grateful to Mr. Van Wyk for doing a superb job, even though I ultimately decided to publish my work in the United States.

The last word of thanks is especially reserved for my family. My research work in South Africa took me away from my wife and three boys for months on end and, after my return, the analysis and writing of research findings added more hours of unavoidable absence from my loved ones. I am very thankful to my wife, Thembi, and sons, Mpumi, Dumi and Siso for their sustaining love, patience and understanding.

The financial assistance of the Centre for Science Development (Human Sciences Research Council, South Africa) is hereby acknowledged. Opinions expressed in this publication and conclusions arrived at are those of the author and are not necessarily to be attributed to the Centre for Science Development.

ABBREVIATIONS

ASB	Afrikaanse Studentebond
ANC	African National Congress
DP	Democratic Party
FF	Freedom Front
GNU	Government of National Unity
IFP	Inkatha Freedom Party
NP	National Party
NUSAS	National Union Of South African Students
PAC	Pan Africanist Congress
RDP	Reconstruction and Development Program
SA	South Africa
SASO	South African Students Organization
UCT	University of Cape Town
UNIN	University of the North
WITS	University of the Witwatersrand
USA	United States of America

Introduction

The arrival of the Dutch settlers in South Africa in 1652 to establish a halfway station for the ships of the Dutch East India Company in their voyages to and from the East marked the beginning of a long history of racial conflict between the indigenous people and whites. The imposition of white rule was resisted by the indigenous people in various ways, including armed struggle. By the early 20th century white domination was firmly established and in 1948 it reached its zenith with the introduction of the system of racial segregation called apartheid.

The system of legalized racism, known world-wide as apartheid, was established in 1948 when the Nationalist Party of the Afrikaners came into power as an ethnic block and began to dominate South African politics. What became formally known as the apartheid system at that point in the history of the country was simply the political culmination and legal codification of white domination which began when the Dutch settled in the country. The system affected every aspect of the South African society; Whites, Coloreds, Indians and Africans were separated and locked into a racially stratified system which was controlled and dominated by the white group. There was sustained opposition to apartheid since its inception in 1948.

The apartheid system was condemned by the international community and resisted vigorously by the oppressed. It also generated intense debate internally as proponents and opponents advanced arguments for or against the status quo. South African universities, as institutions of higher learning and centers of new ideas, became naturally involved in the debate for and against the apartheid system. As important components of the society, they were not immune to the political and ideological currents that affected the rest of the country. The currents can be broadly divided into conservatism, liberalism and the politics of liberation.

In general, the Afrikaans-medium universities were ideologically conservative and politically aligned with and in support of the apartheid system. The Afrikaanse Studentebond (ASB), the organization representing Afrikaner students, was also conservative and supported the status quo. This does not mean, however, that the Afrikaans-speaking students were a politically monolithic group. This was amply demonstrated by events at the University of Stellenbosch in the 1980s when some Afrikaner students there were the first to dissent and openly challenge the apartheid system.

The English-speaking universities were steeped in the tradition of liberalism and were opposed to the apartheid system. The National Union of South African Students (NUSAS), which was multiracial but dominated by whites, was also liberal-oriented and against apartheid. As a national students organization, NUSAS also included members from black universities. These so called black universities were formally established during the apartheid era under the Extension of University Education Act of 1959 which applied the apartheid system to universities. The relationship of NUSAS with these black universities was terminated in 1968 when the exclusively black students organization, the South African Students Organization (SASO), came into being and subsequently severed its connection with NUSAS. SASO was influenced by the militant philosophy of

2

Black Consciousness which was committed to the psychological and physical liberation of black people from white domination. It was the philosophy of Black Consciousness which ultimately inspired the black students who were involved in the Soweto Students Uprising of 1976.

South African university students played an important, historic role in the fight for or against the apartheid system which was finally brought to an end in 1994 when the first all-race elections were held. It is in the aftermath of those historic elections, which marked the beginning of the new South Africa, that the views of students were solicited about power sharing, equality and democracy in the new South Africa.

Key Questions

This study focuses on final year university students and their attitudes toward the concepts of power sharing, equality and democracy in the new South Africa in the aftermath of the country's historic transition from the system of legalized racism known as apartheid to a society based on nonracial and democratic principles.

The government of national unity, which was based on the transitional constitution, was in office in South Africa for about a year when this study was undertaken in 1995. At the core of the new political dispensation was the concept of power sharing, which had been advocated by the political elites as a necessary basis for a united and stable new South Africa. The question was, How did groups other than the political leaders, specifically university students from whose ranks will most likely emerge the future leaders, view power sharing, racial equality, democracy and related issues? To find answers to that question, a number of final year students associated with a cross section of South African universities were asked structured questions. The key questions were classified under twelve major categories.

Power Sharing

Power sharing in the new South Africa meant that the majority party, the ANC, would share political power in a government of national unity with parties that had won at least five percent of the national vote. On the basis of the power sharing agreement several parties were represented in the new cabinet of President Nelson Mandela.

Under the category of power sharing, students were asked the following questions: To what extent were the students in favor of or against power sharing in South Africa? In a racially and ethnically divided country like South Africa, is power sharing a better basis for democracy than outright majority rule? Is power sharing necessary for reconciliation, especially following the first nonracial elections in South Africa? Is power sharing necessary for peace and stability? Should power sharing be limited to five years, the duration of the transitional government of national unity, or should it be extended beyond the limited period of five years? Is power sharing, as a permanent feature of the South African political system, a good idea? Given the fact that the period leading to the first nonracial elections was marked by violence and political intimidation in some parts of the country, to what extent were the students apprehensive about the political future of the new South Africa? Did power sharing contribute to the reduction of political violence after the elections?

Since the concept of power sharing was the main focus of the study, space was provided after the structured questions to enable the respondents to elaborate ad libitum on the advantages and/or disadvantages of power sharing.

Political Parties

Unlike in the past when parliamentary politics was the exclusive domain of white people, in 1994 a number of political parties participated in the first nonracial elections in the history of South Africa. To participate in national elections was a privilege whites had always enjoyed but for the black majority it was a new experience. Apart from the leading contending political parties, the National Party of the former white rulers and the African National Congress of the former liberation movement, there were also a number of other parties, like the Freedom Front and the Inkatha Freedom Party, which contested the elections.

Under the category of political parties, students were asked to state the particular political party they had voted for in the 1994 nonracial elections. Since it can be hypothesized that in South Africa, (where the two major sections of the population are black and white) political choices can be influenced by racial preferences, students were asked if race played any part in the choice of their political group. Moreover, because there are many ethnic groups in South Africa, it can be assumed that political choices can be influenced by ethnic preferences. Hence, students were asked if ethnicity had played any part in the choice of their political group. Were they satisfied with the results of the first nonracial elections in South Africa? Which party would they vote for, if elections were held in 1995? Did they agree that the first nonracial election in the history of South Africa was really about getting rid of apartheid? Did they agree with the statement that the test of the new democracy in South Africa is not the first election but subsequent ones?

Racial Equality

White domination was part and parcel of South African history since the arrival of the Dutch in 1652 and, in 1948, it took the form of apartheid which became the law of the land. In the new South Africa, which began in 1994, all races were considered to be equal under the law.

If, under the law, racial equality is defined as equal treatment of all racial groups, To what extent were the students in favor of or against racial equality? Did blacks in the new South Africa receive equal treatment under the law? Would racial equality be realized in South Africa? How long might it take to realize racial equality in South Africa?

Ethnic Equality

Under apartheid laws, South African society was not only racially stratified, with whites at the top and blacks at the bottom of the racial pyramid, but Africans were also divided into several ethnic groups.

In the new South Africa, ethnic groups, as well as their specific languages, were of equal status under the law.

If all ethnic groups are accorded equal status under the law, then ethnic groups can be said to have ethnic equality. The question then was, To what extent were the students in favor of or against ethnic equality? Did they think that ethnic equality would be realized in South Africa? And how long might it take to realize ethnic equality in South Africa?

Democracy

Whatever the meaning of the word democracy in the South African context before the all-race elections of 1994, it certainly did not mean that Indians, Coloreds and Africans could exercise the right to vote. Until April, 1994, only Whites could participate in national politics. The 1994 elections put an end to the all-white prerogative and democracy was accorded its universally recognized meaning of government by the people, for the people, through their elected representatives.

In a representative multi-party democracy, the adult population has a right to vote with a choice between political parties. To what extent were the students in favor of or against that type of democracy? In a representative one-party system, the adult population has the right to vote for individual candidates within the same party. To what extent were the students in favor of or against such a political system?

Were the students for or against majority rule? Did they believe that absolute majority rule was inevitable in South Africa? Would black majority rule in South Africa amount to black domination? Would black majority rule in South Africa cause white alienation? Would black majority rule result in racial conflict?

Of the three political systems, namely a unitary system, a federal system and a consociational system, which one would the students choose for South Africa? And which one of the three proposed political systems would be ideal for racial harmony in South Africa? Which political system would be ideal for ethnic harmony? Which one would be ideal for democracy? Which political system, if any, should be entrenched in a new South African constitution?

To achieve a broader perspective on the key concepts, further questions were asked about related issues which might have a major impact on power sharing, racial equality and democracy in South Africa. The following were the related issues:

The Economy
The South African economy generates considerable wealth. The country is blessed with gold, diamonds and other rich minerals. But, historically, the wealth of the country was accumulated and monopolized by whites through the exploitation of cheap black labor. The majority of whites were the beneficiaries of the economy and the majority of blacks were disadvantaged by being denied access to the wealth of their native land.

In the sphere of the economy, did the students agree or disagree with the statement that, because of the legacy of apartheid, the majority of whites in South Africa have greater economic power than blacks? How would they categorize the socio-economic gap between whites and blacks in South Africa? What were the expectations of the students about the socio-economic gap between whites and blacks after five years? Did they agree or disagree with the statement that political power sharing does not necessarily mean economic power sharing?

Were the students in favor of or against the distribution of wealth through higher taxes for the rich? Did they agree or disagree with the statement that the state of economic inequality in South Africa had a potential for racial conflict? Were they in favor of or against the policy of the Government of National Unity (GNU), which had put considerable faith in the business sector as the main engine for economic growth and development? Did they agree or disagree that the state of economic inequality in South Africa had a potential for class conflict? Could the Reconstruction and Development Program (RDP) of the government effectively narrow the gap between the rich and the poor in South Africa?
Since capitalism is the norm in South Africa, would the Western style market economy succeed in narrowing the gap between the rich and the poor? Did they think that socialism would be a better system than capitalism in narrowing the gap between the rich and the poor? Should the government resort to nationalization of the commanding heights of the economy to narrow the gap between the rich and the poor in the country?

Was South Africa headed for a major conflict , if the government did not succeed in narrowing the gap between the rich and the poor through the RDP? Would the crime rate soar, if the gap between the rich and the poor was not reduced? Would the climate of peace and goodwill continue, if the government did not succeed in upgrading the socio-economic conditions of black people?

8

Workers

Black workers were historically exploited in South Africa; the gap between white and black workers was wide and maintained through apartheid laws. In the new South Africa, the expectations of black workers for a qualitatively better life are very high and the black majority government is under pressure to improve their economic status.

Were the students for or against the government policy of calling upon the workers to "tighten their belts" in the interest of economic growth and development? Should workers be denied more wages in order to maintain productivity? Would black workers in South Africa wait for economic growth and development before pressing their demands for better wages through strike action? Did students believe that, if there was successful growth and development, employers would voluntarily give workers better wages? Did they favor or oppose strike action by workers? Should employers have the constitutional right to lock out striking workers?

Affirmative Action

The GNU implemented affirmative action to enable blacks to have better opportunities for employment. But the policy of affirmative action in the new South Africa, as in the United States where it originated, is very controversial.

Were the respondents for or against affirmative action? Did they think that affirmative action would serve to portray blacks as unqualified workers? Would white workers be justified in viewing affirmative action as reverse discrimination? Would affirmative action contribute to antagonistic race relations in South Africa?

Education

Historically, because of racism, blacks had to struggle in South Africa to get an education. After the introduction of the apartheid system, education was racially segregated by law and blacks received an inferior education. Only a few succeeded in obtaining a good education beyond the matriculation level.

Did the respondents agree or disagree that the educational system in South Africa needed radical transformation to enable blacks to get a good education? How would they rate the standard of education in black schools? How would they rate the standard of education in white schools? How would they rate the standard of education in traditionally segregated black universities? How would they rate the standard of education in traditionally white universities?

Language

Language is a very complex issue in South Africa. Before the 1994 elections there were only two official languages: English and Afrikaans. African languages were taught in schools but were not recognized as official languages. After the elections, all the African languages were elevated to the same official status as English and Afrikaans. English and Afrikaans still dominate commerce but now share the status of official languages with nine other indigenous African languages.

South Africa is the only country in the world with eleven official languages. Were the respondents in favor of or opposed to the existence of so many official languages? Did they agree or disagree with the statement that the national interests of the country would be better served by one official language? Were they for or against English as the only official language?

Did they think that their own language would be demoted if English would be made the only official language? Were they for or against the holding of a national referendum to recognize English as the only official language in South Africa?

10

Would they accept or reject that national decision, if the majority of South Africans participating in the proposed referendum endorsed English as the only official language? If language is the main vehicle of culture, to what extent would they support the right of different racial and ethnic groups to preserve their own languages?

National Anthem

In apartheid South Africa there was only one national anthem, DIE STEM and it was in the Afrikaans language. The new South Africa has two national anthems i.e. NKOSI SIKELEL 'IAFRIKA/MORENA BOLOKA SECHABA SA HESO of the former liberation movement and DIE STEM of the old South Africa.

To what extent did the respondents favor or oppose the existence of two national anthems in South Africa? To what extent were they in favor of or against one amalgamated national anthem which combined parts from NKOSI SIKELEL "IAFRIKA/MORENA BOLOKA SECHABA SA HESO and DIE STEM?

Leaders

The challenge to the apartheid system, and the task of dismantling it, required courageous leadership from both blacks and whites. On the part of the white power structure, the catalyst to changing entrenched white attitudes would finally come with the leadership of F.W. de Klerk. Liberation of the oppressed was represented by the freeing of Nelson Mandela from jail in 1990. Incarcerated for 27 years for fighting the oppressive system, his release set the stage for an historic negotiated settlement that would change the course of South African history.

In the area of leadership, did the respondents agree or disagree that F.W. de Klerk played a major role in persuading the white electorate to change? Did they agree or disagree that Nelson Mandela had made a major contribution to the struggle for freedom in South Africa? Did they agree or disagree that Nelson Mandela had done much, since his inauguration as president, to restore confidence in democracy

11

in the new South Africa? Did they agree that president Nelson Mandela was the social glue that kept blacks and whites together? To what extent were the respondents apprehensive about the future stability of South Africa after Mandela?

After the primary questions, the respondents were asked general questions relating to their background. The questions covered the following categories:

Age, Gender, Personal or Marital status, Number of Children, Education, Types of Primary and Secondary Schools attended, Majors taken at respective Universities, Religion, Class, Place of Residence and Name of University attended by respondent.

It was determined that questions relating to background information were not critical to the outcome of the study and were therefore omitted from the final evaluation of the research data.

PART I

RESPONSES TO STRUCTURED QUESTIONS

1

POWER SHARING

The first all-racial national elections of April 1994 marked the end of the apartheid era and the beginning of the new South Africa. The Government of National Unity (GNU), which was based on the transitional power sharing constitution and intended to govern for five years, took office after those elections. In accordance with the terms of power sharing, all political parties that gained 5% of the national vote were entitled to take part in the new government of national unity. In the course of the five years during which the GNU would run the country, a final constitution would be drawn up by the duly elected Constitutional Assembly. Several parties were represented in the new cabinet of president Nelson Mandela, including those that did not qualify for seats under the power sharing constitution. At the core of the new political dispensation was the concept of power sharing which was defined as government by consensus among the participating political groups. Power sharing was advocated by the political elites as a necessary basis for the emergingnew South Africa. It was seen as an important framework for legitimacy, the development of political and social institutions to replace apartheid, reconciliation, and future stability. How did groups other than the political elites view the power sharing arrangement? Particularly, how did the university student population, from whose ranks will most likely emerge the future leaders of the new South Africa, think of power sharing? To find an answer, final year university students in nine universities were asked a number of probing questions about power sharing.

The participants were asked: "To what extent are you in favor or against power sharing in South Africa?" Out of a total of 930 respondents, 87% were either strongly or moderately in favor of power sharing, and only 7%, were strongly against the arrangement (Table 1.1).

Table 1.1 Participants in Favor or Against Power Sharing

		Frequency	Percent
Strongly in favor		471	50.6
Moderately in favor		335	36.0
Moderately against		55	5.9
Strongly against		60	6.5
	*	9	1.0
	Total	930	100.0
Valid cases	921	Missing cases	9

* Represents missing cases

Power sharing was not only supported by the respondents but it was also seen as a better basis for democracy than majority rule. To the question, Is power sharing a better basis for democracy than majority rule? 70% of the respondents answered "yes", 12.% answered "no" and 17.% were "uncertain" (Table 1.2).

The endorsement of power sharing as a better basis for democracy than majority rule, however, cannot be interpreted to mean that the respondents were not in favor of majority rule per se. It could simply be a reflection of the general mood of the country at the time. People were in a mood for reconciliation, peace and

16

stability after the oppression, violence and instability which characterized the apartheid era. Before and after the elections, the African National Congress which had emerged victorious in those elections, hammered on the theme of reconciliation and peace as a basis for a stable and peaceful South Africa. That theme of reconciliation, peace and stability is reflected in the answers given by respondents, of whom 73% thought that power sharing was necessary for reconciliation and only 6.% thought it was not necessary (Table 1.3).

Table 1.2   Is Power-Sharing a Better Basis for Democracy?

			Frequency	Percent
Yes			648	69.7
Uncertain			161	17.3
No			114	12.3
		*	7	.8
	Total		930	100.0
Valid cases	923		*Missing cases	7

One year after the first all-race elections, the majority of the respondents were in support of power sharing as a basis for reconciliation. At that point, they had had an opportunity to observe how the different groups were adjusting to the new political dispensation and the overwhelming majority of them arrived at the conclusion that power sharing made a major contribution to reconciliation.

17

Table 1.3   Is Power Sharing Necessary for Reconciliation?

		Frequency	Percent
Yes		674	72.5
Have reservations		197	21.2
No		52	5.6
*		7	.8
	Total	930	100.0

Valid cases   923   *Missing cases   7

Seventy seven percent of the respondents thought that power sharing was necessary for peace (Table 1.4). Before the national elections, there were groups, particularly a minority of right wing Afrikaner elements, that predicted that there would be a major racial conflict in the country after the end of apartheid. In their view, the different racial groups could never have a peaceful coexistence in a unified South Africa and only the apartheid system could serve as a basis for peace. But there was racial peace in South Africa and the majority of respondents concluded that power sharing was necessary for that peace.

Sixty seven percent of the respondents thought that power sharing was also necessary for stability (Table 1.5). The country had to maintain stability if it was to move ahead with development and attract foreign investments. Without development and economic growth the new black majority government would not be able to improve the socio-economic conditions of the poor and would find it difficult to promote peace and reconciliation. The respondents agreed that, for the country to remain stable, the power sharing arrangement was a necessary condition.

18

Table 1.4   Is Power Sharing Necessary for Peace?

		Frequency	Percent
Yes		711	76.5
Have reservations		146	15.7
No		66	7.1
	*	7	.8
	Total	930	100.0
Valid cases	923	*Missing cases	7

Table 1.5   Is Power Sharing Necessary for Stability?

		Frequency	Percent
Yes		619	66.6
Have reservations		204	21.9
No		100	10.8
	*	7	.8
	Total	930	100.0
Valid cases	923	*Missing cases	7

Those high figures in favor of power sharing as a basis for reconciliation, peace and stability dropped down considerably, when two more probing questions relating to the duration of power sharing were raised. Asked if power sharing should be limited to a period of five years, the duration of the transitional government of national unity, the respondents were almost evenly divided: 37% replied "yes" and 43.% said "no" (Table 1.6). The transitional period after apartheid was a critical stage for the new country and power sharing was viewed as a necessary basis for a smooth adjustment . But after that period, power sharing seemed to lose its attractive force.

Table 1.6   Should Power Sharing be Limited to Five Years?

			Frequency	Percent
Yes			339	36.5
Have reservations			169	18.2
No			403	43.3
		*	19	2.0
		Total	930	100.0
Valid cases	911		*Missing cases	19

And looking further into the future, respondents were asked if power sharing should be extended beyond the limited period of five years: 50% said "yes" and 33% said "no" (Table 1.7). The extension is supported by the respondents but with less enthusiasm.

20

Table 1.7   Should Power Sharing be Extended over Five Years?

			Frequency	Percent
Yes			465	50.0
Have reservations			146	15.7
No			305	32.8
			1	.1
		*	13	1.4
		Total	930	100.0

Valid cases	917	*Missing cases	13

Power sharing therefore received overwhelming approval for the transitional period as a basis for reconciliation, peace and stability but there also seems to be some concern about the future of the country as indicated by a slightly higher support for an extension of power sharing over the stipulated period of five years.

This concern about the future of the country is also reflected in responses to the question of whether power sharing should be a permanent feature of the South African political structure: 57% said "yes" and 27% said "no" (Table 1.8).

The role of power sharing in the reduction of political violence was also acknowledged by 53% of the respondents (Table 1.9). Political violence was still a problem, particularly in the province of KwaZulu-Natal, where supporters of the ANC and Inkatha Freedom Party were still vying for political supremacy, but it had subsided or disappeared in other parts of the country. In general, apprehension about the political future of the new South Africa was clearly in the minds of the students as indicated by support for power sharing as a permanent feature of the South African political system (Table 1.10).

21

Table 1.8   Should Power Sharing be a Permanent Feature?

		Frequency	Percent
Yes		528	56.8
Have reservations		151	16.2
No		246	26.5
*		5	.5
	Total	930	100.0

Valid cases   923   *Missing cases   7

Table 1.9   Has Power Sharing Reduced Political Violence?

		Frequency	Percent
Yes		495	53.2
Uncertain		208	22.4
No		220	23.7
*		7	.8
	Total	930	100.0

Valid cases   923   *Missing cases   7

Table 1.10   Aprehension about the Political Future of South Africa

			Frequency	Percent
Very much			198	21.3
To an appreciable extent			241	25.9
To some extent			412	44.3
Not at all			49	5.3
		*	30	3.2
		Total	930	100.0

Valid cases	900	*Missing cases	30

A comparison of the nine universities on the question of power sharing does shed some light on the relative positions of respondents in traditionally black universities and those in traditionally white universities.** In traditionally black universities, the percentages of respondents strongly in favor of power sharing is high and closely corresponds to the combined percentage, 51%, of all nine universities (see Table 1.1). At the University of Fort Hare 51% of respondents were strongly in favor of power sharing. Sixty one percent at the University of the North, and 66% at the University of Zululand were strongly in favor of power sharing. The traditionally black universities therefore were collectively in support of power sharing.

In the case of the traditionally Colored (mixed race) and Indian universities respectively, the percentages fall below the combined 51% of the nine universities. At the university of the Western Cape, 46% of the respondents were strongly in favor of power sharing and at the University of Durban Westville almost the same percentage (45%) were strongly in favor. The same pattern of lower support for power sharing is indicated in the traditionally white universities, both Afrikaans

23

speaking and English speaking, albeit the University of the Witwatersrand scored the highest (48%) amongst white universities and the University of Cape Town the lowest (25%) amongst white universities. Overall, 40% of respondents at both the Afrikaans speaking universities of Stellenbosch and Pretoria were strongly in favor of power sharing.

The pattern indicated in the comparative analysis of the nine universities is that the support for power sharing in the "strongly in favor" category is higher than 50% in the traditionally black universities and lower than 50% in the traditionally white, Indian and Colored universities. It can be hypothesized from these figures that the lesser support for power sharing on the part of traditionally white, Indian and Colored universities had something to do with the fear of minority groups in the face of majority power. This is the power which the apartheid system had tried to neutralize and contain through divide and rule. It was the fear of black majority rule (known otherwise as black peril) which was the dynamic force fueling the apartheid machine. The lower percentages on the part of minority groups seem to underline that residual fear. This fact is even more pointedly underscored in the next question which introduces the concept of majority rule alongside power sharing. When asked if power sharing was a better basis for democracy than majority rule, the combined percentage of all nine universities moved up from the 51%, based on the first question, to a higher level of 70%. That rise of 19% from 51% to 70% is due to the fact that the predominantly white, Indian and Colored universities gave greater support to power sharing as a better basis for democracy than outright majority rule. The University of Cape Town, which registered only 25% "strongly in favor of power sharing", doubled that figure to 56% in support of power sharing as a better basis for democracy than majority rule. The University of the Witwatersrand jumped from 48% to 75%. The University of Pretoria jumped from a mere 40% to 79% and so did the University of Stellenbosch which doubled its support from 40% to 80%. The

24

University of the Western Cape also moved up from 46% to 63% and the University of Durban Westville doubled its support from 45% to 90%.

Of the three black universities, only UNIN moved some points up from 61% to 70%. The other two traditionally black universities had percentages slightly lower than the combined average. The University of Zululand moved down from 66% to 63%, and the University of Fort Hare remained at exactly the same level of 51%.

The general pattern indicated by a comparative analysis of traditionally white and traditionally black universities is that power sharing as a basis for democracy is a more attractive option than majority rule in white, Colored and Indian universities than in traditionally black universities. Majority rule may translate into black majority rule and possibly black domination. Given the historical fact that, during the apartheid era, a white minority had dominated the majority black population, a reversal of roles might have been a major concern on the part of minority groups and hence the reason they found majority rule, as a basis for democracy, a less attractive option.

The necessity of power sharing for reconciliation, peace and stability received consistent and strong support in all nine universities. When considered separately, the respective percentages of individual universities compared very well with the combined percentage. The high percentages underlined the fact that the desire for reconciliation, peace and stability was strong in all the nine universities.

The period prior to and leading to the first all-race elections was marked by widespread violence and political intimidation, but after the elections there was a significant reduction in the level of violence. The responses indicate that power sharing contributed to that reduction. All nine universities were in agreement that power sharing played a significant role in the decrease of political violence.

However, in view of that violence, apprehension was expressed about the political future of the country.

A comparison of the nine universities indicates that, with the exception of the University of Zululand, there was less concern about the political future in traditionally black universities than in the other universities.

At the university of Fort Hare only 9% of respondents were "very much" concerned about the future, compared to the combined figure of 21% of the nine universities. At the University of the North 12% of the respondents were "very much " concerned about the political future of the country. The figure was higher at the University of Zululand where 25% of respondents were "very much" concerned about the political future of the new South Africa. But, given the fact that there was so much political violence in Natal, before and after the elections, that higher figure seems to be reflective of the regional uncertainties in KwaZulu-Natal.

The traditional white universities, as well as the Indian and Colored universities, showed higher levels of apprehension about the political future of the new South Africa than the traditionally black universities. At the University of the Witwatersrand 26% of respondents were "very much" concerned, 20% at the University of Cape Town, 26% at the University of Pretoria and 30% at the University of Stellenbosch. At the University of the Western Cape, those who were "very much" concerned stood at 26% and 29% at the University of Durban Westville.

The question whether power sharing should or should not be limited to a period of five years, during which the GNU would be governing the country, was posed in conjunction with a second question about whether power sharing should or should not be extended beyond the limited period of the stipulated five years. The three traditionally black universities were consistently against limiting power sharing to the five-year period and favored extending it over that limited period. This was also the position of the two Afrikaans-speaking universities which were strongly against limitation of power sharing to five years and in favor of extension. Similarly, both the University of Durban Westville and the University of the Witwatersrand were against limitation to five years and in favor of an extension. The English-speaking University of Cape Town was in support of the idea of limiting power sharing to five years (61%) and against extending it over that period (53%).

The position of the University of the Western Cape was apparently contradictory in that the difference was very small between support for limitation (37%) to the five year period and an extension (41%) over that same period. The reason for the contradiction lies in the fact that even though 37% of the respondents were for limitation, a sizable number, 26%, expressed reservation on the question of limitation. On the other hand, the percentage of reservations on the extension question was much smaller (17%), thus allowing for a higher figure (41%) in favor of an extension over the five year period.

There was also strong support in the nine universities for the idea of power sharing as a permanent feature of the South African political structure. The exceptions were the University of Durban-Westville and the University of Cape Town which were opposed to power sharing on a permanent basis. The University of Durban-Westville was opposed to the idea of a permanent power sharing arrangement (42%), but that opposition was not strong and was counterbalanced by the supporters of the idea (39%). The strongest opposition to the idea of permanent power sharing was registered at the University of Cape Town (66%) where only a very small number (15%) was in support.

It is instructive to compare the relative positions of the two English-speaking universities on the question of permanent power sharing. The University of the Witwatersrand was in support of the idea (43%) but that support was weak, and a sizeable number of respondents (36%) were opposed to it. As already noted, the University of Cape Town was strongly opposed (66%) to permanent power sharing.

The line of demarcation between the English-speaking universities and the Afrikaans speaking universities was pronounced. The University of Pretoria was strongly in support of the idea of permanent power sharing (65%). The support for the idea was even higher at the University of Stellenbosch (70%). However, it is interesting to note that support for the idea of permanent power sharing was also strong in the three traditionally black universities. At the University of the North, 57% of respondents gave their support to the idea; at the University of Fort Hare, support for the idea stood at 61% and at the University of Zululand 71% said yes to permanent power sharing.

These figures apparently indicate that the two historically antagonistic groups in South Africa - Blacks and Afrikaners - had a vested interest in permanent power sharing, whatever their ultimate motives. Whether both groups were acting in the spirit of reconciliation, peace and stability is a moot point. In the final analysis, Blacks could afford to be magnanimous in victory because they were in the absolute majority and the white members of the former ruling class had to be concerned about losing power permanently by dint of their minority status in South Africa. The statistics seem to underscore this political reality.

** Tables of responses from individual universities are not included in this study. They are in the possession of the author and would be made available upon request.

2

POLITICAL PARTIES

In the first all-race elections of April 1994, the ANC emerged as the undisputed winner. This fact is reflected in the political choices made by students who participated in the survey. The respondents voted overwhelmingly for the ANC, 58%, and only 20% for the National Party (the former ruling party of the apartheid era). The leading contenders in those elections were the ANC and the NP, with other parties vying with the NP for second position. The other major party, the Inkatha Freedom Party, received only 3% support from the respondents. The Democratic Party received 4% and the Freedom Front 3% (Table 2.1).

A comparative analysis of the political choices of students associated with the nine universities reveals a differential voting pattern. The predominantly white English-speaking universities voted overwhelmingly for the ANC. At the University of the Witwatersrand, 60% voted for the ANC and 16% for the National Party. At the University of Cape Town, the ANC received 76% of the vote and the NP only 2%. The ANC was clearly the favored party in English-speaking universities.

The ANC also received solid support in traditionally black universities. At the University of the North, the ANC captured 89% of the vote and its rival, the

29

PAC, took a distant second position with 4%, followed by the NP with 2%. At the University of Fort Hare, the ANC took the first position with 72% of the vote and the PAC came a distant second with 9%. At the University of Zululand, the backyard of the IFP, the ANC received 63% of the vote and the IFP was put in a distant 3rd position with 10%, followed by the NP's 9%.

Table 2.1   Political Party Voted for in 1994 Elections

	Frequency	Percent
African National Congress	535	57.5
National Party	186	20.0
Inkatha Freedom Party	29	3.1
Freedom Front	28	3.0
Democratic Party	33	3.5
Pan Africanist Congress	20	2.2
Others	27	2.9
Did not vote	53	5.7
*	19	2.0
TOTAL	930	100.0

Valid cases	911	*Missing cases	19

At the Colored University of the Western Cape, the ANC again emerged as the strongest party with 73%, followed by the NP in second position with 15%. The ANC also received strong, albeit relatively reduced support (55%) at the predominantly Indian University of Durban Westville, where the National Party came in second place with a more respectable slice of the vote (36%) than in the predominantly Colored University of the Western Cape or the traditionally black universities.

30

The generally high support received by the ANC was, however, effectively challenged at both Afrikaans-speaking universities where the NP emerged the clear winner. At the University of Pretoria, the NP won 57% of the vote, followed by the Freedom Party (13%), which campaigned for an apartheid-type political system, and the ANC in the distant third position. At the University of Stellenbosch, the NP was again the winner but with reduced support (40%) followed by the ANC in second position (25%).

The pattern that emerges from the survey of all nine universities would suggest that race and ethnicity did have an impact on the political choices of the respondents. But in the final analysis, even though race might have played a part in the political choices of the respondents, those responding "no" to race outnumbered the "yes" vote by 58% to 40%. (Table 2.2). This pattern was also reflected in the comparative positions of all nine universities viewed separately.

Ethnicity was even more firmly rejected than race by 73% to 25% (table 2.3). The respondents took the position that ethnicity did not play a major role in their choice of political parties. The responses of all nine universities considered separately corresponded to the combined average of all nine universities.

The first nonracial elections in the history of South Africa marked the end of the apartheid order and the dawn of a new political dispensation. The eradication of the hated apartheid system was the dominant factor in those elections. The majority of the respondents (62%) concurred that the first nonracial elections in the history of South Africa were fundamental to abolishing the apartheid system (table 2.4).

Table 2.2   Did Race Play a Part in Political Choices?

	Frequency	Percent
Definitely Yes	147	15.8
Yes	229	24.6
No	370	39.8
Definitely No	168	18.1
*	16	1.7
Total	930	100.0

Valid cases   914   *Missing cases   16

Table 2.3   Did Ethnicity Play a Part in Political Choices?

	Frequency	Percent
Definitely Yes	68	7.3
Yes	164	17.6
No	426	45.8
Definitely No	257	27.6
*	15	1.6
Total	930	100.0

Valid cases   915   *Missing cases   15

Table 2.4   The 1994 Election was about Getting Rid of Apartheid

		Frequency	Percent
Agree		574	61.7
Uncertain		159	17.1
Disagree		193	20.8
	*	4	.4
	Total	930	100.0

Valid cases   926   *Missing cases   4

If the first nonracial elections were about getting rid of an unacceptable political system, could they be also a true test of democracy and would that test be the focus of subsequent elections? Although just a little over half of the respondents (51%) agreed that the test for true democracy would be in subsequent elections, a significant number of respondents (35%) were uncertain about this matter (table 2.5).

Larger majorities in the English-speaking universities of Cape Town and the Witwatersrand and the Afrikaans-speaking universities of Pretoria and Stellenbosch agreed that the true test of democracy is still to come. The position of the Indian University of Durban-Westville corresponded to that of the white universities. Respondents at the Colored University of the Western Cape were almost evenly divided between those who agreed (44%) and those who were uncertain (42%). The same pattern of responses appeared at both the University of the North where 40% agreed and 40% were uncertain. At the University of Fort Hare, 35% were in agreement and 33% were uncertain. However, at the University of Zululand, more respondents (50%) were uncertain and a smaller

33

number (29%) agreed that the true test of democracy would come in subsequent elections.

Table 2.5   The Test of Democracy in South Africa is in Subsequent Elections

		Frequency	Percent
Agree		472	50.8
Uncertain		326	35.1
Disagree		123	13.2
*		9	1.0
	Total	930	100.0

Valid cases   921   *Missing cases   9

Given the fact that at the University of the North and the University of Fort Hare, respondents were almost evenly divided between those who agreed and those who were uncertain, and that at the University of Zululand the majority of respondents were uncertain, was this an indication on the part of black students that they felt a sense of uncertainty about the future of democracy in South Africa?

The question was, How would the respondents vote if elections were to be held a year after the first elections (i.e., when the research survey was conducted in 1995)? The political choices of the respondents indicate that one year later, the ANC still emerged as the most favored party with 48% of respondents declaring their support for it (Table 2.6). But that figure is ten points down from the 58% gained earlier by the organization at election time. The National Party still held to its second position with 21%, which is one point higher than the 20% it received

34

at election time. The support for the ANC decreased consistently in almost all universities, with the exception of the Afrikaans speaking University of Pretoria (8%), where it gained about 2%, and the University of Stellenbosch (30%), where it gained 5%. The largest drops for the ANC were at the University of the Western Cape (from 73% to 64%), the University of the North (from 89% to 68%, the University of Zululand (from 63% to 53% and the University of Fort Hare (from 72% to 51%). At the traditionally liberal University of the Witwatersrand, the ANC also registered a politically significant drop (from 60% to 51%).

Table 2.6   Preference of Political Party in 1995

	Frequency	Percent
African National Congress	444	47.7
National Party	195	21.0
Inkatha Freedom Party	20	2.2
Freedom Front	32	3.4
Democratic Party	39	4.2
Pan Africanist Congress	25	2.7
Others	42	4.5
Would not vote	116	12.5
*	17	1.8
TOTAL	930	100.0

Valid cases	913	*Missing cases	17

Support for the second popular party, the National Party, remained exactly the same and minimal at both the University of the Witwatersrand (16%) and University of Cape Town (2%). At Stellenbosch support for the National Party remained exactly the same at 40%, but at the University of Pretoria, support dropped from 57% to 51%. Support for the National Party also dropped at the University of the Western Cape from 15% to 12% and at the University of Durban-Westville from 36% to 29%. The National Party however gained support at the black University of the North (from 2% to 8%) and at the University of Zululand (from 9% to 17%), but zero support at the University of Fort Hare.

The dramatic drop in black support for the ANC may be an indication that initial high expectations of blacks for an improved life after the elections were dampened by the harsh socio-economic conditions still surrounding them. Blacks were aware that the election promises of the ANC, heralding a higher quality of life, remained largely unfulfilled. Therefore, the drop in black support may indicate dissatisfaction with broken promises. On the other hand, the slight rise in Afrikaner support for the ANC may point to the irrelevance of initial fears Afrikaners had about losing their privileged status. The ANC had reassured Afrikaners that their privileged life was in no real danger. But, the gain in Afrikaner support is small in comparison to the significant drop in black support, and since the black vote is by far the largest entity, that drop means a significant loss in political terms.

3

RACIAL EQUALITY

One of the cardinal principles of the new South African constitution is nonracialism. In the new South Africa, all racial groups are entitled to be treated equally under the law. The results of the survey corroborated this fact.

The majority of respondents (70%) were "definitely in favor" of racial equality under the law (table 3.1). The strongest support for the idea came from the two English speaking universities - the University of the Witwatersrand and the University of Cape Town - and the Indian University of Durban-Westville. Support for the idea of equality in all three universities averaged over 80%. At the University of the Western Cape and the University of Stellenbosch, the support for the idea was at the 70% level. The University of Zululand and the University of the North were also "definitely in favor" of racial equality and both averaged above 65%. The lowest support (51%) came from the University of Fort Hare which was also "definitely in favor" of racial equality. The relatively lower percentage at the University of Fort Hare is however not necessarily an indication that the idea of racial equality was not strongly supported by blacks, because a sizable number of respondents at that university (37%) declared themselves to be "in favor" of racial equality.

Table 3.1   In Favor or Against Racial Equality

	Frequency	Percent
Definitely in favor	649	69.8
In favor	229	24.6
Against	20	2.2
Definitely against	27	2.9
*	5	.5
Total	930	100.0

Valid cases   925   *Missing cases

Table 3.2   Do Blacks Receive Equal Treatment in the New South Africa?

	Frequency	Percent
Yes	229	24.6
Uncertain	288	31.0
No	404	43.4
*	9	1.0
Total	930	100.0

Valid cases   921   *Missing cases   9

To recognize and accept the idea of racial equality specified by law did not, however, mean that blacks were receiving equal treatment. In the survey 43% of the respondents stated that blacks were still not receiving equal treatment under the law, and 31% were uncertain whether blacks were in fact receiving equal

38

treatment under the law. Only 25% of the respondents thought that in the new South Africa blacks were receiving equal treatment under the law (table 3.2).

Viewed separately, most universities either did not support the idea that blacks received equal treatment under the law or projected an uncertain opinion in line with the combined average of all universities. All three black universities, as well as the Indian University of Durban Westville and the University of Cape Town, were adamant that blacks were not receiving equal treatment under the law. At the Colored University of the Western Cape more students were uncertain (39%) about the issue of racial equality under the law than those who said there was no equal treatment under the law (32%). At the University of the Witwatersrand, respondents were evenly divided between those who said there was no equal treatment (39%) and those who said they were uncertain (39%). At the University of Stellenbosch, respondents were evenly divided between those who said blacks received equal treatment (40%) and those who said they did not receive equal treatment (40%). Only the University of Pretoria (46%) took the position that blacks were treated equally under the law, but here, too, a sizable number (33%) said blacks were not receiving equal treatment under the law.

Looking more into the future, the majority of respondents (43%) said that it was possible for racial equality to be realized. A smaller, but significant number (32%), said they were doubtful that racial equality could ever be realized. Only a small number (16%) said racial equality would be realized in the new South Africa (Table 3.3).

Table 3.3   Will Racial Equality be Realized in South Africa?

		Frequency	Percent
Yes		152	16.3
Possibly		396	42.6
Doubtful		295	31.7
No		82	8.8
	*	5	.5
	Total	930	100.0

Valid cases	925	*Missing cases	5

The same pattern of responses regarding the future of racial equality emerged in almost all the universities considered separately. The only exceptions were Durban-Westville, where more respondents were doubtful (36%) about racial equality being realized than those who said it could possibly be realized (32%), and the University of Fort Hare where more were doubtful (40%) about racial equality than those who said it could possibly be realized (35%).

Asked to state the numbers of years it would take racial equality to be realized in the new South Africa, the majority of respondents (38%) projected that it would take "decades" before racial equality could be achieved (Table 3.4). A significant number (29%) also felt that it would take "years".

This pattern of responses is repeated in almost all universities viewed separately, except at Fort Hare where a higher number of respondents (37%) thought it would take "years" and a smaller number (23% said it would take "decades", and the University of Zululand where a higher number (36%) thought it would take

40

"years" and a smaller number (29%) said it would take "decades" before racial equality could be attained in the new South Africa.

Table 3.4   Estimated Time for the Realization of Racial Equality

			Frequency	Percent
Years			271	29.1
Decades			352	37.8
A century			106	11.4
Two or more centuries			71	7.6
Never			122	13.1
		*	8	.9
	TOTAL		930	100.0
Valid cases	922	*Missing cases		8

The views of respondents regarding the state of racial equality in the new South Africa and their projections about the time needed to implement equality, reflect the stark socio-economic inequities. These disparities between rich and poor, primarily between whites and blacks, illustrate that, even though the concept of equality under the law has become a political reality, economic justice is still a distant dream in South Africa.

4

ETHNIC EQUALITY

The South African population under the apartheid regime was divided and segmented by law, not only along racial lines, but also along ethnic lines. The question was, therefore, If all ethnic groups are accorded equal status under the law, to what extent were the respondents in favor of or against ethnic equality?

A near majority (48%) were "definitely in favor" and a slightly smaller but significant number (42%) were just "in favor" of ethnic equality (Table 4.1). That pattern of being "definitely in favor" or just "in favor" of ethnic equality was repeated throughout all nine universities viewed separately without exception. However, to point out that respondents strongly supported the idea of ethnic equality is not the same as saying that ethnic equality will be realized in the new South Africa.

To the question " Do you think that ethnic equality will be realized in South Africa?" 38% of respondents thought it could "possibly" be realized and 34% thought it was "doubtful" that it would be attained in the new South Africa (Table 4.2).

In all the predominantly white universities, as well as the Indian and the Colored universities, those who thought that ethnic equality could "possibly" be realized

43

in the new South Africa were higher than those who were "doubtful". The situation was reversed in all three black universities where the number of those who were "doubtful" about the realization of ethnic equality was higher than those who thought that it could "possibly" be realized.

Table 4.1   In Favor or Against Ethnic Equality

	Frequency	Percent
Definitely in favor	450	48.4
In favor	391	42.0
Against	65	7.0
Definitely against	12	1.3
*	12	1.3
Total	930	100.0

Valid cases	918	*Missing cases	12

In the ethnic stratification system of the old apartheid South Africa, blacks were relegated to the very bottom level of society. In the new South Africa, their ethnic position has been legally validated in accordance with the new constitution, but, for the overwhelming majority of blacks, the reality of their daily existence has not changed significantly, if at all. That may explain the doubts emanating from black universities regarding the realization of ethnic equality in the new South Africa.

Table 4.2   Will Ethnic Equality Be Realized in South Africa?

			Frequency	Percent
Yes			145	15.6
Possibly			350	37.6
Doubtful			316	34.0
No			110	11.8
		*	9	1.0
	Total		930	100.0

Valid cases   921   *Missing cases   9

The doubts expressed by blacks aside, what did the respondents think about the length of time it might take to realize ethnic equality in the new South Africa? Thirty five percent of the respondents thought it might take decades and 28% thought it might take years (Table 4.3).

The same pattern is repeated at the different universities with the exception of the University of Fort Hare (37%) and the University of Zululand (37%). Both had a higher number of respondents who thought it might take "years" instead of "decades."

Since the respondents at both the University of Fort Hare and the University of Zululand were "doubtful" about the realization of ethnic equality, it would have been more logical for the majority of them to have opted for the "decades" rather than the "years" category, but, the respective positions of both the University of Fort Hare and the University of Zululand are in line with earlier positions taken on racial equality. On both racial and ethnic questions, both black universities opted for the "years" category rather than the "decades" one. Their doubts about

45

the realization of ethnic equality should therefore be seen in terms of "years" rather than "decades".

Table 4.3   Estimated Time for the Realization of Ethnic Equality

		Frequency	Percent
Years		260	28.0
Decades		322	34.6
A century		116	12.5
Two or more centuries		76	8.2
Never		144	15.5
	*	12	1.3
	TOTAL	930	100.0
Valid cases	918	*Missing cases	12

The overall results relating to the ethnicity question indicate that ethnic equality, as with racial equality, may be a legal fact in the new South Africa but it may take a long time before emerging as a social reality. The results also point to a clear recognition by all respondents that the wide socio-economic gap between blacks and whites in the new South Africa does not in any way correspond to the legal principle of ethnic and racial equality proclaimed in the constitution. In other words, the new South Africa, despite the new legal order, is still an ethnically and racially divided and stratified society and may remain as such for years or decades to come.

46

5

DEMOCRACY

The first nonracial elections of April 1994 in South Africa involved a number of different political parties, both large and small, that spanned the ideological spectrum from the extreme left to the extreme right. The competition for political power was carried out in the context of a representative multiparty democracy relating to a population that can exercise the right to vote, with a choice between political parties.

The question was to what extent were the respondents in favor or against such a type of representative multiparty democracy. A high number of respondents (57%) were "strongly in favor" and a smaller number (37%) was just "in favor" of such a type of democracy (Table 5.1).

Similar views were expressed at the different universities viewed separately. The only exception was the University of Fort Hare where more respondents (54%) were just "in favor" of and fewer (37%) were "strongly in favor" of such a political system. In other words, the majority of students at the University of Fort Hare were in favor of the idea but did not feel as strongly about it as respondents at other universities.

Table 5.1   In Favor or Against Representative Multiparty Democracy

	Frequency	Percent
Strongly in favor	527	56.7
Moderately in favor	343	36.9
Moderately against	28	3.0
Strongly against	17	1.8
*	15	1.6
TOTAL	930	100.0

Valid cases   915   *Missing cases   15

One political system that has never been tried but has been implemented in other African countries is a representative one-party system in which the population has the right to vote for individual candidates within the same party. The question that respondents were asked in relation to that system was, To what extent were they in favor of or against such a political system?

In the combined results of all nine universities, 35% were "in favor" of, 18% "definitely in favor" of and the rest, almost equally divided between those who were against (22%) and those who were "strongly against" (23%) (table 5.2). There is a higher percentage of those "in favor" of but the rest of the results are more or less evenly distributed. However, an interesting picture emerges when the different universities are considered separately.

Table 5.2   For or Against a Representative One-Party System

		Frequency	Percent
Definitely in favor		171	18.4
In favor		321	34.5
Against		200	21.5
Strongly against		213	22.9
	*	25	2.7
	TOTAL	930	100.0

Valid cases   905   *Missing cases   25

At the University of Cape Town, 32% were "against", 27% "strongly against", 25% "in favor" and 14% "definitely in favor". There was therefore more opposition to a one-party system at the University of Cape Town. At the University of the Witwatersrand 38% were "strongly against", 27% "against", 21% "in favor" and 10% 'definitely in favor". Therefore, at both English-speaking universities the overall picture that emerges is that a greater number of students were opposed to a one-party political system than supported it.

At the University of Stellenbosch, the results were virtually evenly distributed amongst those who were "definitely in favor" (25%, those "in favor" (25%), those "against" (25%) and those "strongly against" (20%). The overall picture here indicates a very small preference for such a system.

At the University of Pretoria there were even more of those "in favor" (41%) and a slightly smaller number of those who were "definitely in favor" (20%). Only 20% were "strongly against" and 17% "against." There was a greater preference for such a one-party system at this university .

At both Afrikaans speaking universities, therefore, respondents showed an unexpected preference for a one-party system. This preference was startling, given the fact that one-party systems have always been associated with communism - an ideology that was stigmatized and outlawed during the apartheid regime. Also a great deal of the anti-liberation propaganda of the Nationalist Party focused relentlessly on the failures of one-party states in the rest of Africa. The ANC was projected in Nationalist Party propaganda as the party that would introduce communist dictatorship in South Africa because of its links with the Communist Party of South Africa and ultimately with Moscow. And so for respondents who had earlier indicated that they had voted for the Nationalist Party during the April 1994 elections and that they would vote for it again if elections were held one year later, it is quite interesting that they showed some preference for a one-party system.

At the University of Durban-Westville, despite the fact that there was a higher number of respondents who were "in favor" (32%) and very few (10%) who were "definitely in favor", the total picture that emerges (58%) favors a combination of those who were "against" (29%) and those who were "strongly against" (29%).

At the University of the Western Cape, the majority of respondents were "in favor" (35%) and "definitely in favor" (22%). On the opposing side, 28% were "against" and 14% were "strongly against" a one-party system. The overall results therefore favor those who supported a one-party system.

All the black universities showed strong support for a one-party system. At the University of Fort Hare, 51% of respondents were "in favor" of and 9% "definitely in favor" of a one-party system. Only 21% were "against" and 9% "strongly against." At the University of Zululand, 38% were "in favor" and 23% "definitely in favor" as compared to 18% who were "against" and 17% "strongly against." Here, again, we have an indication of a greater preference for a one-party

50

system. At the University of the North, 32% of respondents were "in favor" and 21% "definitely in favor" of a one-party system. Nineteen percent were "against" and 27% "strongly against" such a system. Again a preference for a one-party system prevailed.

Therefore, out of the nine universities that were surveyed, only three were opposed to a one party system, notably the two English-speaking universities and the Indian University of Durban-Westville.

In trying to make sense of why so many respondents expressed a preference for a one-party political system, one can only surmise that students were distancing themselves from a system that has a great potential for internecine conflict and fragmentation. It has been pointed out very eloquently by supporters of a representative one-party system, most notably Julius Nyerere of Tanzania, that a one-party political system is more suitable for the African countries where ethnicity has a negative impact on the political process because people there tend to vote along ethnic lines. In South Africa, the groups that were affected the most by ethnic and racial divisions were blacks and Afrikaners: blacks because they were on the receiving end of racial domination and ethnic segmentation (apartheid); and Afrikaners because they were members of the dominating race whose role was to maintain white supremacy at all costs. If these historically hostile and antagonistic groups have to find common ground, away from racial divisions and ethnic polarization, it would make perfect sense that they would prefer a one-party political system where the focus would be on the merits of individual candidates rather than party platforms which are bound to be perceived through racial and/or ethnic prisms. More light should be cast on this question as other aspects of the study relating to the democratic process are analyzed.

The question of democracy was put to the test vis-a-vis the concept of majority rule. If the principle of majority rule is universally accepted as an integral part of

51

the democratic process, to what extent was that idea favored or opposed by the respondents?

In the combined results of all nine universities, 44% of the respondents supported majority rule, 39% had reservations and 16% were against the principle (Table 5.3). Given the fact that less than 50% of respondents were in favor of majority rule, the question remains, Why is there lukewarm support for such a universally recognized principle? The answer could be found in a comparative analysis of the respective positions of the different universities.

Table 5.3   For or Against Majority Rule

	Frequency	Percent
For	413	44.4
Have reservations	362	38.9
Against	148	15.9
*	7	.8
TOTAL	930	100.0

Valid cases	923	*Missing cases	7

All three black universities gave favorable and solid support to the principle of majority rule: 62% at the University of Zululand, 61% at the University of the North and 58% at the University of Fort Hare. There was also major support for the concept at the University of the Western Cape (54%) and the University of Cape Town (59%). At the University of Durban-Westville, only 42% supported the idea and 39% had reservations. At the University of the Witwatersrand there were more reservations expressed (53%) than favorable support (33%) for the idea.

52

The only opposition to the concept of majority rule was registered at the Afrikaans-speaking universities. At the University of Stellenbosch, 45% of the respondents had reservations, 30% were opposed, and only 25% were in favor of majority rule. At the University of Pretoria, 51% of respondents had reservations, 38% were opposed and only 11% were in support of the idea of majority rule. The question is, Why are there reservations about and opposition to the principle of majority rule?

In view of the fact that blacks in South Africa are in the majority, Were the Afrikaner respondents viewing majority rule in black and white terms to the extent that for them majority rule translates willy-nilly into black majority rule? At any rate, since blacks make up the majority of the population, Is black majority rule not inevitable in South Africa, simply from a mathematical point of view?

On the question of the inevitability of absolute black majority rule, the combined results of the nine universities indicate that a significant number of respondents expressed uncertainty (43%) about that idea. There was however a little over a third (35%) who believed that absolute majority rule is inevitable in South Africa (Table 5.4). The only universities which deviated from this general pattern and agreed that absolute black majority rule is inevitable in South Africa were the University of Stellenbosch where 35% said "yes" to the idea and 30% were "uncertain", and the University of Durban-Westville, where 45% said "yes" and 42% were "uncertain."

If there is general uncertainty about the inevitability of absolute black rule, there is still overall agreement that black majority rule will amount to black domination (43%); thirty percent of the respondents were 'uncertain" about the idea (Table 5.5). A different picture emerges when the nine universities are considered separately.

53

Table 5.4   Is Absolute Black Majority Rule Inevitable in South Africa?

		Frequency	Percent
Yes		329	35.4
Uncertain		399	42.9
No		187	20.1
	*	<u>15</u>	<u>1.6</u>
	TOTAL	930	100.0

Valid cases	915	*Missing cases	15

At both English-speaking universities, respondents did not think that black majority rule would amount to black domination, although in both places a sizable number were "uncertain" that would be the case. At the University of Cape Town, 44% said "no" to the inevitability of black domination and 34% were "uncertain" and, at the University of the Witwatersrand, 38% said "no" and 37% were "uncertain." At the University of the Western Cape, 35% did not think that black rule would translate into black domination, but a third (33%) were "uncertain" about that eventuality. At the University of Fort Hare, 37% were "uncertain" and a smaller but significant number (35%) said "no" to the idea of black domination. At the University of Zululand, the respondents were almost evenly split between those who were "uncertain" (35%) and those who said (34%) black rule will end up in black domination.

Table 5.5   Will Black Majority Rule Amount to Black Domination?

		Frequency	Percent
Yes		397	42.7
Uncertain		281	30.2
No		246	26.5
	*	6	.6
	TOTAL	930	100.0

Valid cases	924	*Missing cases	6

The rest of the universities said "yes" to the statement that black rule will amount to black domination: at the University of the North 39% said "yes" and 30% were "uncertain"; at the University of Durban-Westville 52% said "yes" and 29% were "uncertain"; at the University of Stellenbosch 60% said "yes" and 25% were "uncertain'; and at the University of Pretoria 72% said "yes" and 21% were "uncertain." Clearly the highest numbers believing in black domination were at the Afrikaans-speaking universities followed by the Indian university of Durban-Westville.

It is not surprising that the numbers are so high in the Afrikaans-speaking universities because the whole philosophy of apartheid revolved around the propaganda axis of black peril (swaart gevaar, in Afrikaans). The rationalization of the ideology of racial separation (apartheid) was predicated on the premise that the separation of the races was necessary to avoid domination of one group by another. Since blacks far outnumbered whites, the domination that the apartheid system was supposedly trying to neutralize or prevent was black domination. This could explain why such a significantly high number of Afrikaner respondents thought black rule could amount to black domination.

The Afrikaners, however, did get some support for their position from the University of the North where 39% of the respondents declared that black majority rule would translate into black domination, even though 31% said "no" to the idea and 30% were "uncertain." The belief in the idea at the University of the North that black majority rule may end up in black domination does indicate that the Afrikaner response may not be far fetched after all, and that the attitude projected could not be dismissed as baseless or irrational. The possibility of black domination is also supported to some extent by a number of blacks who impart credibility to the viewpoint of Afrikaner respondents.

The question is, If black majority rule does become a reality, how will whites, who were once the exclusive rulers of blacks, adjust to that new political order? Would black majority rule cause white alienation?

In the combined results, about a third of respondents said "possibly"; about a quarter, 23%, said "no"; 22% said "yes"; and 21% were "doubtful" that whites could be alienated by black majority rule (Table 5.6).

The opinions on this question varied widely when the different universities were considered separately. At the English-speaking universities of Cape Town and the Witwatersrand, respondents were of the view that black majority rule could "possibly" cause white alienation (41% at the Univ. of the Witwatersrand, 42% at the Univ. of Cape Town). At the Afrikaans-speaking universities the respondents also took the position that white alienation could "possibly" be caused by black majority rule (41% at the Univ. of Pretoria, 45% at the Univ. of Stellenbosch). There was, however, more concern in the Afrikaans-speaking universities than in the English-speaking ones. In the former, the number of those who said "yes" there would be white alienation was high (Univ. of Pretoria 45%, Univ. of Stellenbosch 35%). In both English-speaking universities, the "yes" responses were below 20% (Univ. of Wits 17%, Univ. of Cape Town 5%).

56

Table 5.6   Will Black Majority Rule Cause White Alienation?

		Frequency	Percent
Yes		201	21.6
Possibly		311	33.4
Doubtful		193	20.8
No		217	23.3
	*	8	.9
	TOTAL	930	100.0

Valid cases   922   *Missing cases   8

At the Indian University of Durban-Westville, a comparatively high percentage of respondents (61%) said black majority rule could "possibly" cause white alienation. At the University of the Western Cape a little less than a third of students were "doubtful" (30%) that black majority rule could cause white alienation, and those who thought that white alienation could "possibly" happen (27%) equaled those who said "no" (27%) to the idea of white alienation.

In the black universities, less concern regarding the question of white alienation was registered. At the University of Zululand, 29% of respondents were "doubtful" that white alienation could take place and this figure is very close to those who said there would be no (28%) white alienation. At the University of the North, a higher number of respondents said there would be no (32%) white alienation caused by black majority rule, 27% said it could "possibly" happen followed by those who were "doubtful" (25%) that white alienation would happen. The highest number of those who said there would be no (42%) white alienation was registered at the University of Fort Hare and this number was followed by those who were "doubtful" (28%) about the whole idea.

57

If black majority rule could "possibly" cause white alienation, is it then conceivable that it could also result in racial conflict. The question of whether black majority rule would result in racial conflict elicited different responses from the respondents. The combined results indicate that 32% of respondents thought that it was possible that black majority rule would result in racial conflict. A smaller number (27%) said black majority rule would result in racial conflict and others (25%) said there would be no racial conflict (Table 5.7). But taken separately, the universities projected different positions once again.

At the University of the Witwatersrand, 40% of the respondents said that black majority rule would "possibly" result in racial conflict, but, at the University of Cape Town, 42% of the respondents said it was "doubtful" there would be racial conflict while 32% said it could "possibly" happen. At the University of Stellenbosch, 35% said it was possible and an equal number , 35%, said there would be racial conflict. At the University of Pretoria an even higher number of respondents, 56%, said there would be racial conflict and 36% said it could "possibly" occur. At the University of Durban-Westville, 45% thought that racial conflict could "possibly" take place. At the University of the Western Cape, 33% thought racial conflict could "possibly" materialize.

At the black universities the relatively higher numbers relate to those who are "doubtful": 32% at the University of the North and 35% at the University Fort Hare. At the University of Zululand, 36% of respondents said there would be no racial conflict.

Table 5.7   Will Black Majority Rule Result in Racial Conflict?

			Frequency	Percent
Yes			247	26.6
Possibly			297	31.9
Doubtful			150	16.1
No			230	24.7
		*	6	.6
	TOTAL		930	100.0

Valid cases	924	*Missing cases	6

Therefore, on the black side of the equation, the only university that unambiguously took the position that there would be no racial conflict is the University of Zululand. On the white side, the only university that unequivocally said there would be racial conflict is the University of Pretoria. It is instructive that the two opposite positions are taken by a predominantly black university and a primarily Afrikaner university reflecting, as it were, the opposite views of the former oppressed class and the former ruling class respectively. At any rate, in the final analysis, the nearly 60% combination of the "yes" and "possibly" values underlines the majority viewpoint expressed by the respondents that black majority rule would result in racial conflict (Table 5.7)

Prior to the historic April 1994 elections that marked the end of apartheid, and following those elections, there was much discussion throughout the country about the nature of the political system that should replace the old order. The three major political systems proposed for South Africa were a unitary structure where political power is centralized, a federal structure where power is decentralized and devolved to the nine provinces, and a consociational structure

59

where executive power is shared by the elites of the various racial and ethnic groups (e.g. English, Afrikaners, Coloreds, Indians, Zulu's, Soothes etc.) that have communal autonomy and can exercise mutual vetoes to protect their interests. In view of this national debate, the respondents were accordingly asked to choose one political system of their preference.

In the combined results, there was a higher preference for a unitary system (43%), followed in the second place by a federal system (36%), and in the third place a consociational system (18%) (Table 5.8).

Table 5.8   Preference of a Political System

	Frequency	Percent
Unitary system	397	42.7
Federal system	334	35.9
Consociational system	170	18.3
*	29	3.1
TOTAL	930	100.0

Valid cases   901   *Missing cases   29

The same general pattern of preferences for the three political systems was followed by the two English speaking universities of the Witwatersrand (47%, 34%, 17%) and Cape Town (61%, 34%, 2%). Likewise, the same pattern and order of preference was reflected at the University of the Western Cape (65%, 21%, 12%%) and Durban-Westville (39%, 36%, 26%). The latter, University of Durban-Westville, did not actually register a distinctly pronounced preference for a unitary system because the difference in percentages of preference for a unitary

60

state and federal state is very small. All three black universities also followed the same general pattern of greater preference for a unitary state followed closely in second position by a federal system: the University of Zululand (46%, 35%, 15%; the University of Fort Hare (42%, 30%, 19%); and the University of the North (58%, 25%, 15%). It is only in the Afrikaans-speaking universities where a marked departure from the general pattern of preferences is found.

Both the University of Pretoria and the University of Stellenbosch showed a higher preference for a federal political system. At the University of Stellenbosch 75% of respondents preferred a federal system, followed by 15% who opted for a unitary system. At the University of Pretoria, 54% of respondents chose a federal system, followed by 31% of those who preferred a consociational system.

The results for the Afrikaans-speaking universities clearly indicate that, on the one hand, a unitary political structure was less popular in the case of Afrikaner respondents because, for them, it actually meant loss of power. On the other hand, a federal structure was very popular with Afrikaner students because it meant decentralization, devolution and, therefore, retention of some political power. And since the Afrikaner respondents had already indicated that they would be dominated by the black majority, it certainly makes sense for them to prefer a political system that would minimize the possibility of that black domination. Such a scenario takes us back to the question of race. If there is indeed the possibility of racial domination in the new South Africa, should efforts not be directed towards realizing a political system that should be ideal for non domination and, therefore, better for race relations?

All three political systems were evaluated in terms of their support for racial harmony. The question was, Which political system would be ideal for racial harmony in South Africa? The overall results indicate that a unitary state was the first choice, albeit at a reduced level (37%), followed in the second position (29%)

61

by a federal structure, and in third position (19%) a consociational system (Table 5.9).

Table 5.9   Which Political System Would be Ideal for Racial Harmony?

	Frequency	Percent
Unitary system	340	36.6
Federal system	273	29.4
Consociational system	176	18.9
None	119	12.8
*	22	2.4
TOTAL	930	100.0

Valid cases   908   *Missing cases   22

A comparative analysis of the different universities indicates that all black universities opted for a unitary structure as an ideal system for racial harmony in South Africa.   The English-speaking universities and the University of the Western Cape also had a high preference for a unitary structure.   The Indian University of Durban-Westville chose a federal structure (32%), followed by a unitary system (29%). There is not much difference in percentages at Durban-Westville in terms of a preference for a unitary or a federal system.

On the related question of ethnicity, the combined responses indicate a greater preference for a unitary structure (31%) but also a significant preference for a federal system (28%) and a consociational system (25%). The difference in percentages in the three choices is clearly not large due to the impact of differential patterns of choice associated with individual universities (Table 5.10).

62

Table 5.10   Which Political System Would be Ideal for Ethnic Harmony?

		Frequency	Percent
Unitary system		291	31.3
Federal system		260	28.0
Consociational system		231	24.8
None		132	14.2
	*	16	1.7
	TOTAL	930	100.0

Valid cases   914   *Missing cases   16

A unitary state followed by a federal state was the first choice of both English-speaking universities and the three black universities. The rest of the universities had a different combination of choices. At the University of the Western Cape, a high number of respondents chose a unitary structure (47%) but had minimal preference for either a federal or consociational system. At the University of Durban-Westville there was a greater preference for a consociational system (39%), followed by a unitary system (29%). Both Afrikaner universities gave minimal support to a unitary system. Fifty five percent at the University of Stellenbosch preferred a federal system and 37% at the University of Pretoria chose a consociational system. The unitary political system, therefore, featured prominently in seven out of the nine universities but received very little support in the two Afrikaans-speaking universities.

The debate about and preference for the three political systems relates in the final analysis to the fundamental question of the compatibility of each system to a democratic political dispensation. The question was which political system would be ideal for democracy in South Africa?

63

The responses to that question closely mirrored the questions on race and ethnicity. In the combined results the unitary system was the first choice (41%), followed by a federal system (31%) (Table 5.11). That pattern was reflected in the two English-speaking universities, the three black universities and the University of the Western Cape. At the University of Durban-Westville there was a slightly greater preference for a federal system (36%) than for a unitary system (32%). At both Afrikaans-speaking universities the federal system was the first choice for democracy.

A constitutional endorsement would be required for any of the three political systems to be made a permanent feature of the South African political scene. In answer to the question about which of the three systems should be entrenched in the new constitution, the combined results followed the same pattern of greater preference for a unitary structure (36%) and lesser, albeit significant, preference for a federal system (29%) (Table 5.12).

Table 5.11   Which Political System Would be Ideal for Democracy in South Africa?

	Frequency	Percent
Unitary system	381	41.0
Federal system	290	31.2
Consociational system	153	16.5
None	87	9.4
*	19	2.0
TOTAL	930	100.0

Valid cases   911   *Missing cases   19

Table 5.12   Which Political System Should Be Entrenched in South Africa?

	Frequency	Percent
Unitary system	335	36.0
Federal system	273	29.4
Consociational system	184	19.8
None	111	11.9
*	27	2.9
TOTAL	930	100.0

Valid cases   903   *Missing cases   27

Both English-speaking universities followed the same pattern with even a larger support for a unitary system. The three black universities and the University of the Western Cape joined the English-speaking universities in the same pattern of responses. The University of Durban-Westville gave first preference (36%) to a federal system and second (29%) to a unitary system. Both Afrikaans-speaking universities gave first and greater support to a federal system and second and lesser support to a consociational system.

One more time, a unitary structure featured prominently in the majority of universities and a federal structure received major support from the two Afrikaans-speaking universities and, to a lesser extent, from the Indian University of Durban-Westville.

The respondents in the black universities preferred the idea of a unitary state because blacks are in the majority and would not easily lose their political power. Also, for blacks, having suffered for so long under a system that was segmented along both racial and ethnic lines, a unitary system would represent a reversal of the old political order and therefore a better political system.

In the case of Afrikaners, and to some extent Indians, being a minority would influence them more in the direction of a federal system or consociational structure, both of which allow for the division and devolution of political power.

6

THE ECONOMY

The apartheid system had as much to do with political domination as with economic deprivation. Whites were favored and protected by the system while blacks were made to suffer. After the demise of apartheid, the continuing impact of the legacy of white domination became of paramount importance. The question is whether, because of the legacy of apartheid, the majority of whites in South Africa have greater economic power than blacks. On this question, there was a high degree of agreement on the part of all respondents when considered together (82%) (Table 6.1).

Seven universities viewed separately - three black, two English, one Colored and one Indian - scored above the combined average of 80%. The two Afrikaans-speaking universities also agreed with the statement that the majority of whites had greater economic power than blacks, but their percentages were less than the collective average of 80.0% (75% for Stellenbosch and 60% for Pretoria). The rest of the Afrikaner respondents in both universities were divided between those who were "uncertain" or "disagreed." But these dissenting voices were certainly smaller than those who agreed that whites in post-apartheid South Africa had more economic power than blacks. Apart from those minor differences, the majority of Afrikaner students expressed views that were in line with the seven other universities.

67

Table 6.1   Do the Majority of Whites Have Greater Economic Power than Blacks?

		Frequency	Percent
Agree		762	81.9
Uncertain		92	9.9
Disagree		72	7.7
	*	4	.4
	TOTAL	930	100.0

Valid cases   926   *Missing cases   4

There was certainly strong agreement in all nine universities regarding the economic advantages that the majority of whites have because of the legacy of apartheid, but there were differences of opinion about how to quantify the economic gap between whites and blacks. In the combined results, 55% of the respondents indicated that the socio-economic gap between whites and blacks is "very large" and about half that figure (26%) thought the gap was just "large." In other words, a combination of 81% thought the gap was "large" and "very large" (Table 6.2).

Table 6.2   The Socio-Economic Gap Between Blacks and Whites in South Africa

			Frequency	Percent
Very large			511	54.9
Large			239	25.7
Medium			125	13.4
Small			32	3.4
Very small			17	1.8
		*	6	.6
	TOTAL		930	100.0
Valid cases	924	*Missing cases		6

All the universities viewed separately, with the exception of the University of Pretoria, made similar choices and described the economic gap as "very large" in the first instance and just "large" in the second place. At the University of Pretoria, the first choice was the "large" category (38%) followed by the "medium" (31%) and, in the third place, the "very large" category (22%). The second Afrikaans-speaking university, the University of Stellenbosch, agreed with the other universities that the economic gap between whites and blacks was "very large" (45%) and "large" (30%).

The future economic gap between whites and blacks could not be definitively predicted by the respondents but, asked to speculate on this question in terms of their general expectations, the results were widely spread out, albeit less pessimistic. In the whole sample, 25% of the respondents said the gap would be "large" and 31% predicted that the gap would be "medium." Those who said the gap would still be "very large" (17%) equaled those who thought the gap would be small (17%) (Table 6.3).

Table 6.3   Estimated Socio-Economic Gap in Five Years

			Frequency	Percent
Very large			153	16.5
Large			236	25.4
Medium			287	30.9
Small			156	16.8
Very small			92	9.9
		*	6	.6
	TOTAL		930	100.0

Valid cases	924	*Missing cases	6

The results were similarly spread out when different universities were considered separately. In general, the English-speaking universities opted for the "large" category and so did the Colored, Indian and one black university (Fort Hare). The two Afrikaans-speaking universities and two black universities (University of the North and University of Zululand) chose the "medium" category in speculating about the future economic gap between whites and blacks. In general, the results relating to the future were closely divided among the five choices and not indicative of a very clear pattern largely because of the speculative nature of the question. However, a combination of 42% estimated a "large" and "very large" gap in five years.

The respondents may not have been absolutely clear about what the future held in store for post-apartheid South Africa, but there was general agreement, with small

70

variations, that political power sharing did not necessarily translate into economic power sharing. For the whole sample, although some were "uncertain" (24%) and others chose to "disagree" (21%), the majority agreed (55%) with the statement that political power sharing does not necessarily mean economic power sharing (Table 6.4).

Table 6.4   Political Power Sharing is not Economic Power Sharing

		Frequency	Percent
Agree		507	54.5
Uncertain		222	23.9
Disagree		196	21.1
	*	5	.5
	TOTAL	930	100.0

Valid cases	925	*Missing cases	5

The English-speaking universities agreed in stronger terms than all the other universities (at UCT 76% and at WITS 76%) and so did the Indian University of Durban-Westville (68%). The University of Zululand also agreed with the statement, albeit with less enthusiasm (45%). A significant number was either "uncertain" 27%) or simply disagreed (27%). At the University of Fort Hare there was actually more uncertainty (37%) than agreement (35%) with the statement.

What the results at the two black universities indicate is that political power can be the basis for economic empowerment because it was an historically well-known fact that when Afrikaners finally triumphed in 1948 as a block, they used their new found political clout to improve and elevate the economic status of the Afrikaner people. Therefore, the respective positions of the two black universities may suggest that there is hope on the part of blacks that their political strength will be the springboard for black economic empowerment. That, however, is a minority viewpoint not shared by the majority of respondents who do not believe that political power sharing will necessarily translate into economic power sharing.

How to bring about economic equity in a system that is characterized by huge economic disparities becomes the imperative question. One of the ways of closing the gap between the haves and the have-nots, or bringing about equitable distribution of wealth, is through higher taxes aimed at the rich. Students were asked to address this issue.

The sample results, in response to the question regarding the distribution of wealth through higher taxes for the rich, elicited a mixed reaction from the respondents. However, the overall picture shows that 53% of the respondents are in favor of redistribution of wealth through taxation and 46% are against such a proposition (Table 6.5).

That general pattern becomes altered when the respective positions of the different universities are scrutinized separately. The pattern becomes much clearer if the "definitely in favor" and "in favor" categories are viewed collectively as affirmative and the "definitely against" and "against" categories as negative. Looked at from that perspective, respondents at both English-speaking universities were more in favor of higher taxes for the rich (63% at WITS and 70% at UCT) and so were the respondents at the University of Durban-Westville (65%) and the University of the Western Cape which registered the highest approval rate of 72%.

Table 6.5   In Favor or Against Distribution of Wealth through Higher Taxes

		Frequency	Percent
Definitely in favor		197	21.2
In favor		296	31.8
Against		235	25.3
Strongly against		191	20.5
	*	11	1.2
	TOTAL	930	100.0

Valid cases	919	*Missing cases	11

In the case of the black universities, two were in favor of higher taxes (66% at UNIN and 56% at Fort Hare). At the University of Zululand, the results were almost evenly divided between those in favor of higher taxes (49%) and those against taxing the rich (50%). The Afrikaans-speaking University of Pretoria was firmly against higher taxes for the rich (76%) and, to some extent, also the University of Stellenbosch (50% against and 46% in favor).

The majority of universities, with the exception of the University of Zululand which projected an ambivalent position, and the Afrikaans-speaking universities which were against higher taxes, were in favor of the distribution of wealth through higher taxes for the rich.

Given the state of gross economic disparities between whites and blacks in South Africa, could there be a potential for racial conflict in that state of affairs? If there were some dissenting voices on the question of higher taxes for the rich, there was general agreement on the part of all universities that the current state of economic inequality in South Africa has a potential for racial conflict (65% agreed and 26% were uncertain) (Table 6.6).

Table 6.6   Economic Inequality in S. Africa has Potential for Racial Conflict

			Frequency	Percent
Agree			603	64.8
Uncertain			245	26.3
Disagree			71	7.6
		*	11	1.2
	TOTAL		930	100.0

Valid cases	919	*Missing cases	11

That pattern is repeated in all the universities viewed separately.   On the point regarding the potential for racial conflict, the percentages of each university were above sixty, with the sole exception of the University of the Western Cape where 51% of the respondents agreed and 42% were uncertain.

There is therefore no question that the preponderance of views point to the fact that, unless the socio-economic gap is bridged between the rich and the poor (i.e. between whites and blacks), there would be a great potential for racial conflict in South Africa. That fact is recognized by the majority of the respondents, although not all of them would agree on the usage of the weapon of taxation to close that gap.

Since, under apartheid, South Africa was divided by law along racial lines, it is perhaps understandable that there is great concern about the possibility of a racial conflict, if the wide gap between whites and blacks is not closed. What is also of

74

equal importance is the concern that the current state of economic inequality in the country has the potential for class conflict. In the sample results, 64% of the respondents agreed that there is also a potential for class conflict in South Africa (Table 6.7). It is interesting to note that these percentages are very similar to the ones on the potential for racial conflict. Also, all the individual universities indicated that there is indeed a potential for class conflict, if present economic inequities continue.

Table 6.7   Economic Inequality in S. Africa Has Potential for Class Conflict

		Frequency	Percent
Agree		593	63.8
Uncertain		243	26.1
Disagree		85	9.1
*		9	1.0
	TOTAL	930	100.0
Valid cases	921	*Missing cases	9

The policy of the Government of National Unity (GNU) was to rely on the business sector as the main engine for economic growth and development. Put simply, if there was growth and development, then more jobs would be created for blacks who would then be in a better position to improve their economic status. For that to happen also meant that the business sector would not be handicapped by higher taxes. In the opinion of the GNU, to impose a greater tax burden on the private sector would amount to killing the goose that lays the golden egg. The question was, How exactly was that policy of the GNU being viewed by the respondents?

For the whole sample, there was a slim majority in support of that policy (49%) while a sizable number (44%) had reservations about it (Table 6.8). That pattern of near majority support, along with a significant number of reservations, was repeated throughout the different universities, with the exception of the University of Cape Town where more respondents had reservations (58%) reservations and 34% in favor) and the University of the Western Cape (49% reservations and 42% in favor). The University of Pretoria was split on this issue (47% in favor and 47% reservations).

Table 6.8   For or Against the GNU's Faith in the Business Sector

		Frequency	Percent
In favor		458	49.2
Have reservations		407	43.8
Against		54	5.8
*		11	1.2
Total		930	100.0

Valid cases   919   *Missing cases   11

Overall, the policy of the GNU, which had put considerable faith in the business sector as the great generator of growth and development, did not seem to receive that much enthusiastic support from the respondents. If anything, the significant expression of reservations seemed to point at some strong element of doubt and skepticism about the whole policy.

This doubt and skepticism is reiterated with regard to the potential effectiveness of the Reconstruction and Development Program (RDP) in narrowing the gap between the rich and the poor in South Africa. A higher number of respondents

76

(42%) stated that it was "possible" that the gap could be narrowed and a lower but significant number (32%) were "doubtful" that the RDP could deliver, and only a small number (13%) believed the gap between the rich and the poor could be reduced by the RDP. An almost equal number (13%) said the RDP would in fact not be able to deliver (Table 6.9).

Table 6.9   Will the RDP Narrow the Gap Between the Rich and the Poor?

		Frequency	Percent
Yes		118	12.7
Possibly		390	41.9
Doubtful		296	31.8
No		119	12.8
*		7	.8
	TOTAL	930	100.0
Valid cases	923	*Missing cases	7

That pattern of responses was repeated in the Universities of Cape Town, Witwatersrand, Western Cape, Durban -Westville and the North. At the two Afrikaans-speaking universities, the respondents thought it was more "doubtful" than "possible" for the gap to be narrowed through the RDP (Pretoria 38% doubtful, 32% possible and Stellenbosch 45% doubtful, 40% possible). Two black universities were in agreement with this line of thought (Fort Hare 44% doubtful, 30% possible and Zululand 36% doubtful and 34% possible).

The common denominator in all the universities was the small number of those who thought the RDP could narrow the economic gap, compared to those who were "doubtful" or said it was just "possible" that the gap could be reduced.

77

What would be the possible consequences for the new South Africa if the RDP does not succeed in narrowing the gap between the rich and the poor? Would the country be headed for a major conflict if that happened? Many respondents saw conflict as "possible " (45%) and a smaller number (25%) believed a major conflict would actually ensue (Table 6.10).

That pattern of responses was repeated at the majority of individual universities. There were two exceptions to this general pattern: the University of Cape Town where a high number of respondents (49%) said it was "possible", a significant number (27%) said it was "doubtful" and a smaller number (12%) said there would be a major conflict; the second university to depart from the general norm was the University of Stellenbosch where a higher percentage of respondents (40%) were "doubtful" that there would be such a major conflict and a smaller number (35%) said it was "possible."

Therefore, with the notable exception of the University of Stellenbosch where respondents were more 'doubtful", all the universities were in agreement that it was "possible" that there could be a major conflict if the government fails to bridge the economic chasm between the rich whites and the poor blacks through the RDP.

Table 6.10   If the RDP Fails will there Be a Major Conflict in South Africa?

		Frequency	Percent
Yes		232	24.9
Possibly		419	45.1
Doubtful		178	19.1
No		88	9.5
	*	13	1.4
	TOTAL	930	100.0

Valid cases	917	*Missing cases	13

The level of crime in South Africa has been very high and one of the contributory factors could be related to the rampant poverty typical of the black section of the population. So the question is, Would the crime rate soar if the gap between the rich and the poor is not reduced? In answer to that question, the respondents in the combined results said that "yes" (46%) the crime rate would soar and a significant number (31%) said it was "possible" the crime rate would rise (Table 6.11).

The individual universities followed the same pattern with two exceptions: the University of Stellenbosch and the University of Durban-Westville. At both places, higher numbers of respondents said it was "possible", and lower numbers said the crime rate would go up. The other small deviation was at the University of Fort Hare where the same number of respondents (33%) opted for both the "yes" and "possible" categories.

Table 6.11   Will the Crime Rate Soar if the Economic Gap is not Reduced?

	Frequency	Percent
Yes	425	45.7
Possibly	287	30.9
Doubtful	109	11.7
No	94	10.1
*	15	1.6
TOTAL	930	100.0

Valid cases	915	*Missing cases	15

South Africa's transition from a racist to a democratic society was hailed as a political miracle in many parts of the world and there is no question about it that the April 1994 nonracial elections ushered a period of relative peace and good will into the country. The continuation of that peace and goodwill, however, depends on the solution of structural inequities and ultimately on the success of the government in upgrading the socio-economic conditions of blacks. The important question is whether that climate of peace and goodwill will continue if the government is not successful in uplifting the living conditions of the majority of poor blacks.

In the combined results of the survey, the majority of the respondents (52%) said the climate of peace and goodwill would not continue and 31% were "uncertain" about the outcome (Table 6.12). This pattern of responses was followed by almost all the universities. The only exception and deviation from that general norm was the University of the Western Cape where more respondents were "uncertain" (45%) and fewer (31%) said the climate of goodwill would not continue.

80

Table 6.12   If the GNU Fails will the Climate of Peace & Goodwill Continue?

		Frequency	Percent
Yes		144	15.5
Uncertain		289	31.1
No		480	51.6
	*	17	1.8
	TOTAL	930	100.0

Valid cases	913	*Missing cases	17

In the final analysis, a lot depends on how decisively the government deals with black poverty and ultimately in narrowing the socio-economic gap between whites and blacks. However, South Africa being a capitalist country, the assumption can be made that the eradication of black poverty would have to take place within the context of that economic system. The question then arises whether the Western style market economy can succeed in narrowing the gap between the rich and the poor in that country.

The responses to that question were equally divided between those who said it was "possible" (38%) and those who said it was "doubtful" (38%) that the country would be able to deal with the problem. Only a very small number of respondents (9%) said the Western style economy would succeed in narrowing the gap between the rich and the poor (Table 6.13).

Table 6.13   Will the Western-style Market Economy Narrow the Economic Gap?

		Frequency	Percent
Yes		80	8.6
Possibly		353	38.0
Doubtful		350	37.6
No		135	14.5
*		12	1.3
	TOTAL	930	100.0

Valid cases	918	*Missing cases	12

In almost all universities, considered separately, the results were split between a higher percentage of the "possible" and the "doubtful", with the exception of the University of Zululand, which had more respondents who were "doubtful" (42%) and fewer who said it was "possible" (33%). The University of Fort Hare also had more who were "doubtful" (58%) than those who said it was "possible" (23%) that capitalism would narrow the gap between the rich and poor.

If there is such low confidence in the inherent ability of the Western style market economy to bridge the gap between the rich and the poor the question then arises, Should the government resort to nationalization of the commanding heights of the economy to realize that objective? Although a good number of respondents said "yes" (26%) and an almost equal number said "no" (26%) to nationalization, a higher number of respondents (46%) were "uncertain" whether nationalization would help in reducing the gap between the rich and poor (Table 6.14, p. 83).

Table 6.14   Should the Government Resort to Nationalization to Narrow the
Gap?

		Frequency	Percent
Yes		245	26.3
Uncertain		431	46.3
No		238	25.6
.		1	.1
	*	_15_	_1.6_
	TOTAL	930	100.0

Valid cases	915	*Missing cases	15

Five universities followed that pattern of responses: the three black universities,
the University of the Western Cape and the University of Cape Town. The four
other universities: the English-speaking University of the Witwatersrand, the two
Afrikaans-speaking Universities of Pretoria and Stellenbosch and the Indian
University of Durban-Westville, had higher numbers of those who said "no" to
nationalization than those who were "uncertain."

Nationalization of the commanding heights of the economy may or may not be
associated with the ideology of socialism, which is opposed to capitalism, but the
general perception is that nationalization is associated with that left-wing
economic system.   The question then arises, since the respondents were
"doubtful" about the effectiveness of capitalism in bridging the chasm between the
rich and poor in South Africa, Did they think that socialism would be a better
economic system in doing what capitalism is unable to do?

The sample results regarding the role of socialism in improving the condition of the poor were mixed. With a slightly higher number of those who said it was "possible" and a lower number of those who said "yes", the respondents seem to give socialism a better chance than capitalism to reduce the gulf between the rich and the poor (Table 6.15).

In the case of the individual universities, the "possible" category is given the highest position by two black universities (Fort Hare and Zululand), the Indian University of Durban-Westville, the Colored University of the Western Cape and the University of Cape Town. The University of the Witwatersrand and the two Afrikaans-speaking universities of Pretoria and Stellenbosch gave the "No" category the highest rating. Only the black University of the North gave the highest rating, "yes", to the socialism category (40%) followed in second place by "possibly" (28%).

Table 6.15   Can Socialism Do Better than Capitalism in Narrowing the Gap?

	Frequency	Percent
Yes	226	24.3
Possibly	278	29.9
Doubtful	209	22.5
No	208	22.4
*	9	1.0
TOTAL	930	100.0

Valid Cases   921   *Missing cases   9

Despite the dismal performance of Communist states in Eastern Europe and the collapse of communism in general, it was interesting to note the favorable support

84

for socialism. The general consensus is that socialism can do better than capitalism in narrowing the gap between the rich and poor in South Africa. Also, only white universities said "no" to socialism and one black university said "yes" to socialism.

7

WORKERS

The Government of National Unity embarked on the path of economic growth and development and, in the process, called upon workers, particularly the historically disadvantaged blacks, to tighten their belts in the interest of realizing that major objective. The question was whether the participants in the survey were for or against that policy.

In the overall results, the policy received majority support (58%) from the respondents (Table 7.1). However, two universities - the University of the Witwatersrand and the University of the Western Cape - were "uncertain" about such a policy.

The majority of the respondents (68%) were against denying workers more wages in order to maintain productivity (Table 7.2). None of the nine universities were prepared to support a policy of belt tightening which would involve a denial of more wages to workers in order to maintain high productivity.

It is interesting to note that, even though respondents were generally in support of a belt tightening policy, they were opposed to the implementation of that policy in the area of wages. Perhaps the respondents sensed that such a policy was bound to be challenged by the militant black workers. Hence, the majority of the

87

respondents (66%) took the collective position that workers in South Africa would not wait for economic growth and development before pressing their demands for better wages through strike action (Table 7.3).

Table 7.1   For or Against GNU's Policy for Workers to Sacrifice for the Economy

		Frequency	Percent
For		537	57.7
Uncertain		248	26.7
Against		136	14.6
	*	9	1.0
	TOTAL	930	100.0

Valid cases	921	*Missing cases	9

Table 7.2   Should Workers Be Denied More Wages for Higher Productivity?

		Frequency	Percent
Yes		126	13.5
Uncertain		160	17.2
No		632	68.0
	*	12	1.3
	TOTAL	930	100.0
Valid cases	918	*Missing cases	12

Taken separately, all the universities supported the idea that workers would not wait for economic growth and development before making demands for more wages through strike action.

Table 7.3   Will Workers Wait for Economic Growth before Strike Action?

			Frequency	Percent
Yes			53	5.7
Possibly			87	9.4
Doubtful			169	18.2
No			611	65.7
		*	10	1.1
	TOTAL		930	100.0

Valid Cases   920   *Missing cases   10

Asked whether they were for or against strike action, 39% of respondents had "reservations" and 32% agreed with strike action (Table 7.4). Taken separately, 43% of respondents at the University of the Witwatersrand and 46% at the University of Cape Town supported strike action. At the University of Pretoria, 58% of respondents said "no", and at the University of Stellenbosch 45% were opposed to strike action.

Table 7.4   In Favor or Against Strike Action

		Frequency	Percent
Yes		293	31.5
Have reservation		360	38.7
No		245	26.3
	*	32	3.4
	TOTAL	930	100.0

Valid cases	898	*Missing cases	32

In the event of strikes taking place, should employers have the constitutional right to lock out striking workers? In the combined responses 30% said "yes" and 48% said 'no" to such a constitutional right (Table 7.5). Seven universities followed that same pattern of disagreeing with such a constitutional right. The only two exceptions to that general pattern were the two Afrikaans-speaking universities: at the University of Pretoria (77%) and, at the University of Stellenbosch (45%) the respondents said employers should have the constitutional right to lock out workers.

If workers are not prepared to wait for growth and development before striking out, could employers themselves be expected voluntarily to give workers better wages after successful growth and development? The respondents expressed no clear majority viewpoint in answer to this question. Their overall views ranged from the position that it is "possible" (32%) or "doubtful" (26%) to "yes" (24%) or "no" (16%) (Table 7.6).

90

Table 7.5   Should Employers Have the Right to Lock Out Workers?

		Frequency	Percent
Yes		280	30.1
Uncertain		186	20.0
No		446	48.0
	*	<u>18</u>	<u>1.9</u>
	TOTAL	930	100.0

Valid cases	912	*Missing cases	18

Table 7.6   Would Employers Volunteer Wage Increase?

		Frequency	Percent
Yes		225	24.2
Possibly		300	32.3
Doubtful		243	26.1
No		146	15.7
	*	<u>16</u>	<u>1.7</u>
	TOTAL	930	100.0

Valid Cases	914	*Missing cases	16

The most common viewpoint in all the universities is the "possible" category. At the University of the Witwatersrand, a larger number of respondents (36%) opted for the "doubtful" category. The results were similar at the University of the North where 30% were "doubtful" about such voluntary action on the part of employers. At the University of Cape Town, 39% of respondents disagreed with the idea that employers would volunteer to give better wages to workers after a period of successful growth and development.

8

AFFIRMATIVE ACTION

To correct the historical imbalance in employment between blacks and whites, the Government of National Unity resorted to the policy of Affirmative Action to enable blacks to have better opportunities for employment. The respondents were accordingly asked if they were for or against affirmative action.

In the combined results of the survey, the respondents were either "strongly in favor" (38%) or just "in favor" (35%) of affirmative action (Table 8.1). A much clearer picture is obtained when respondents from individual universities are considered separately.

At the University of Stellenbosch, even though very few respondents (5%) were "strongly in favor" of affirmative action, a high number (55%) were "in favor" of it. At the University of Durban-Westville, more respondents were "strongly against" (32%) and fewer were "in favor" (29%) or "strongly in favor" (23%). Also at the University of Pretoria, there were more respondents who were "strongly against" (37%) or just "against" (34%) affirmative action than those who were "in favor" (21%) of it. The University of Durban-Westville and the University of Pretoria were the only ones that were "strongly against" affirmative action.

93

Table 8.1   In Favor or Against Affirmative Action

	Frequency	Percent
Strongly in favor	356	38.3
In favor	322	34.6
Against	127	13.7
Strongly against	104	11.2
*	21	2.3
TOTAL	930	100.0

Valid cases	909	*Missing cases	21

The statistical picture that emerges from the relative positions of the different universities on affirmative action is that the English-speaking universities, the black universities and the Colored University of the Western Cape were "strongly in favor" of affirmative action to correct historical injustices. The support for affirmative action by English-speaking universities was in line with the liberal traditions of these institutions. The positions of black universities and the Colored university reflected the need for equity by economically disadvantaged and racially oppressed groups.

The University of Stellenbosch, by taking the position of being just "in favor," formed a bridge or transition to the University of Pretoria and the University of Durban-Westville, the two universities that were "strongly against" affirmative action. The position of Durban-Westville on affirmative action was problematic because Indians in South Africa were also historically oppressed, despite the existence of a relatively successful merchant class. It can therefore be hypothesized that the strong opposition to affirmative action in that institution represented the views of a privileged subgroup than the economically

94

disadvantaged group. Overall, it is interesting to note that there was more opposition to affirmative action in universities serving groups that were more economically privileged than blacks. This clearly implies that there was more concern about the impact of affirmative action on the relatively more privileged economic status of these groups.

Opposition to affirmative action revolves mainly around issues of qualifications and skills and not the fundamental question of closing the wide gap between the more privileged and less privileged groups. In practical terms, it may mean bypassing someone with more qualifications and better skills for some one with less such qualities. As a result, the question had to be asked whether affirmative action serves the unintended purpose of portraying blacks as unqualified workers in the eyes of white workers.

In the survey the overall results indicate that the responses to that question were split three ways. There were slightly more respondents who said affirmative action would not portray black workers as unqualified workers (36%) than those who said (33%) blacks would indeed be viewed as being unqualified workers. The rest of the respondents (29%) were "uncertain" about how black workers would be perceived (Table 8.2).

The analysis of responses relating to the individual universities gives a different picture. At the English-speaking University of the Witwatersrand, 42% of the respondents said blacks would be seen as unqualified and a slightly lower number (35%) said blacks would not be viewed as unqualified workers. The results, however, were reversed at the University of Cape Town where a larger number of respondents (58%) disagreed with the statement that blacks would be seen as unqualified workers and a smaller number (32%) were "uncertain" about how affirmative action would impact the image of blacks.

Table 8.2   Affirmative Action Portrays Black Workers as Unqualified

		Frequency	Percent
Yes		309	33.2
Uncertain		272	29.2
No		330	35.5
	*	19	2.0
	TOTAL	930	100.0

Valid cases	911	*Missing cases	19

At the University of the Western Cape, a larger percentage (37%) said "no" to the idea of blacks being viewed as unqualified because of affirmative action, 32% said "yes" and 31% were "uncertain." At the University of Durban-Westville, a larger number of respondents (48%) were "uncertain" and a smaller number (39%) said blacks would be regarded as being unqualified.

At the two black universities, Fort Hare (67%) and the University of the North (55%) the respondents said "no" to the statement and at the University of Zululand more respondents were "uncertain" (45%) about the idea while 27% said "no." At the Afrikaner University of Pretoria, 68% of the respondents, and at the University of Stellenbosch 65% said black workers would be regarded as being less qualified.

The results relating to individual universities indicate that there was more opposition to affirmative action in Afrikaans-speaking universities because of the issue of the qualification of blacks.

There is also the issue of fairness at stake in the application of affirmative action. Someone in the traditionally privileged group may have to be bypassed to give an

96

opportunity to a member of the traditionally underprivileged group. So the question had to be raised whether white workers, in the event of white persons missing opportunities because of the hiring of black workers, would be justified in viewing affirmative action as reverse discrimination.

In the whole sample, the respondents were almost evenly divided between those who thought that (37%) white workers would be justified to think there was reverse discrimination and those who said (38%) white workers would not see affirmative action in that light (Table 8.3).

Table 8.3   Will Whites View Affirmative Action as Reverse Discrimination?

		Frequency	Percent
Yes		343	36.9
Uncertain		221	23.8
No		349	37.5
	*	17	1.8
	TOTAL	930	100.0

Valid cases	913	*Missing cases	17

The positions of individual universities on this question of reverse discrimination, when viewed separately, differed substantially. Both English-speaking universities said "no" to the idea that white workers would be justified in viewing affirmative action as reverse discrimination. Similarly, at the University of the Western Cape, the University of the North and the University of Fort Hare, respondents did not think that affirmative action is reverse discrimination. At the University of Zululand, more respondents (44%) were "uncertain" about the question of reverse discrimination than said "no." The three universities where respondents said "yes"

97

to the idea that affirmative action is reverse discrimination are the University of Durban-Westville (61%), the University of Pretoria (79%) and the University of Stellenbosch (50%). These are the same three universities that did not view affirmative action in a positive light.

In South Africa, as well as in the United States, affirmative action cannot but be viewed through the prism of race because in both countries it involves correcting historical injustices suffered by blacks at the hands of whites. The question therefore had to be asked whether affirmative action would contribute to bad race relations in South Africa.

In the combined responses the results were mixed and respondents were evenly divided between those who said (36%) affirmative action would contribute to bad race relations and those who said it would not (35%). A significant number (28%) were "uncertain" about the overall impact of affirmative action on race relations (Table 8.4). A clearer picture, however, emerges when responses from each individual university are tabulated separately.

In the case of English-speaking universities, at the University of the Witwatersrand, a slightly higher number of respondents (46%) said affirmative action would not instigate hostile race relations and a smaller but significant number of respondents (36%) were "uncertain" about its impact. At the University of Cape Town, 41% of respondents were "uncertain" and a smaller number said there would be no instigation of antagonistic race relations because of affirmative action.

Table 8.4   Will Affirmative Action Contribute to Bad Race Relations?

		Frequency	Percent
Yes		333	35.8
Uncertain		256	27.5
No		325	34.9
	*	16	1.7
	TOTAL	930	100.0

Valid cases	914	*Missing cases	16

At the Colored University of the Western Cape, more students (37%) said affirmative action would not cause bad race relations and a smaller number (32%) said affirmative action would lead to bad race relations.

All the three black universities said "no" to the idea that affirmative action would contribute to adverse race relations. The universities where respondents said affirmative action would contribute to bad race relations in South Africa were the universities of Pretoria (78%), Stellenbosch (60%) and Durban Westville (52%). These three universities were consistent in their negative response to affirmative action.

9

EDUCATION

Education was a major instrument used by the white power elites during the apartheid era to keep blacks in a subordinate status. In the new South Africa blacks have been promised better education. But to enable them to get a good education would the education system in South Africa not have to undergo radical transformation?

In both the combined results and the separate ones, the respondents strongly agreed or otherwise just agreed that the educational system in South Africa needs radical transformation to enable blacks to get good education. Overall, in the sample results, 92% of the respondents were in agreement that the educational system must undergo radical transformation (Table 9.1). In all the separately evaluated universities, the numbers of respondents who strongly agreed were in all cases higher than those who simply agreed.

All the responses indicate that if there was a category of schools that needed radical transformation that category would have to apply to black schools whose educational standards were deliberately lowered by the apartheid regime. In the combined results of the survey the standard of education in black schools was rated by the respondents to be either "poor" or "very poor." Overall, 78% of the respondents agreed that the standard of education in black schools was of a poor

101

quality (Table 9.2). Unlike the rest of the other universities which had higher percentages for the "poor" category and lower ones for the "very poor" one, the universities of Zululand, Durban Westville and Cape Town gave higher numbers to the "very poor" category than to the "poor" one.

Table 9.1   Educational System in South Africa Needs Radical Transformation

		Frequency	Percent
Strongly agree		619	66.6
Agree		236	25.4
Disagree		33	3.5
Strongly disagree		27	2.9
*		15	1.6
	TOTAL	930	100.0

Valid cases   915   *Missing cases   15

Poor education for blacks is one of the most devastating legacies of the apartheid system.   Historically, education for blacks was always inferior in quality and poorly funded by the white power structure. But, when Bantu education (i.e. education for blacks only), was introduced under the apartheid system, educational standards in black school dropped drastically to their lowest level. It was made crystal clear by the advocates of the new educational system that black children were not entitled to the same quality education as white children. If black children received the same education as white children, they were likely to have high aspirations that could not be met in a system that was committed to white supremacy. Bantu education was therefore a major tool to keep blacks permanently in a subservient position. The respondents were aware of that fact, as indicated by their poor rating of black schools

102

Table 9.2   The Standard of Education in Black Schools

			Frequency	Percent
Excellent			11	1.2
Good			28	3.0
Fair			149	16.0
Poor			376	40.4
Very poor			346	37.2
		*	20	2.2
	TOTAL		930	100.0
Valid cases	910	*Missing cases		20

The poor rating of black schools in the combined results contrasts very sharply with the rating of white schools which were considered either to be "excellent" or "good"; both categories added up to a rating of 90% (Table 9.3).

In the separately evaluated results, all three black universities, the Colored University of the Western Cape and the University of Cape Town gave first preference to the "excellent" category followed by the "good" category. The University of the Witwatersrand and the University of Pretoria gave first preference to the "good" category followed by the "excellent" category. The only exception was the University of Stellenbosch which gave first preference to the "good" category followed by the "fair" one.

Table 9.3   The Standard of Education in White Schools

		Frequency	Percent
Excellent		459	49.4
Good		379	40.8
Fair		62	6.7
Poor		8	.9
Very poor		5	.5
	*	17	1.8
	TOTAL	930	100.0
Valid cases	913	*Missing cases	17

Like black schools, the black universities, as compared to white universities did not fare any better during the apartheid era. In the combined results of the study these institutions of higher learning were rated by the respondents to be either "fair" or "poor" (Table 9.4). The same pattern was repeated in all three black universities, the two Afrikaans-speaking universities of Pretoria and Stellenbosch, the University of the Witwatersrand and the University of the Western Cape. The University of Cape Town gave first preference to the "poor" category followed in the second place by the "fair" category. Only the University of Durban Westville gave first preference to the "fair" category followed in the second place by the "good" category.

Table 9.4   The Standard of Education in Traditionally Black Universities

			Frequency	Percent
Excellent			19	2.0
Good			107	11.5
Fair			355	38.2
Poor			281	30.2
Very poor			141	15.2
		*	27	2.9
	TOTAL		930	100.0
Valid cases	903	*Missing cases		2

Again, as in the case of the comparison between black and white schools, there is a sharp and marked contrast between the evaluation of black universities and white universities. In the combined results, white universities were rated either as "excellent" or "good" and these categories added up to a total of 91% (Table 9.5). This pattern is repeated in all black universities, the University of the Western Cape and the University of the Witwatersrand (the latter had 46% for both "excellent" and "good" categories). The Universities of Cape Town, Pretoria, Stellenbosch and Durban-Westville gave first preference to the "good" category followed in the second place by the "excellent" category.

105

Table 9.5   The Standard of Education in Traditionally White Universities

		Frequency	Percent
Excellent		434	46.7
Good		408	43.9
Fair		52	5.6
Poor		8	.9
Very poor		4	.4
	*	24	2.6
	TOTAL	930	100.0

Valid cases	906	*Missing cases	24

10

LANGUAGE

Under white domination, South Africa had two official languages: Afrikaans and English. In the new South Africa, these two languages are just two amongst an unprecedented number of eleven official languages as a result of elevating the indigenous African languages to the category of official languages. Since South Africa is the only country in the world with eleven official languages, the respondents were asked to state to what extent they were in favor or against so many official languages.

In the combined results, a higher number of respondents were either "in favor" (33%) or "strongly in favor" (26%), adding up to a total favorable rating of 56% (Table 10.1). A similar pattern of responses emerged from the University of Cape Town, the University of the Witwatersrand, the University of the Western Cape and the three black universities where the respondents were "in favor" of and "strongly in favor" of the existence of eleven official languages.

A slightly different picture, however, emerged in the University of Durban-Westville and the two Afrikaans-speaking universities of Pretoria and Stellenbosch. At the University of Durban-Westville, although a number of respondents (32%) were "in favor" of eleven official languages, the next significant number of respondents (23%) relates to those who were against the existence of eleven official languages. At the University of Pretoria, the same picture emerges where 28% were "in favor" and 27% were against eleven official languages. At the University of Stellenbosch more respondents (45%) were against and fewer (40%) were "in favor" of eleven official languages.

Table 10.1   In Favor or Against the Existence of Eleven Official Languages

		Frequency	Percent
Strongly in favor		241	25.9
In favor		303	32.6
Uncertain		118	12.7
Against		140	15.1
Strongly against		111	11.9
	*	17	1.8
	TOTAL	930	100.0
Valid cases	913	*Missing cases	17

It is one thing to have so many official languages in such a relatively small country like South Africa but quite another matter whether the overall interests of the country are better served by such an arrangement. The views of students were solicited on this question.

In the overall results a slightly higher number of respondents (31%) "agreed" and a lower number (23%) "strongly agreed" with the statement that the national interests of the country would be better served by one official language but a significant number (28%) disagreed with the statement (Table 10.2). A majority of 54% of the respondents agreed that the needs of the country would be better served by one official language.

108

Table 10.2   One Official Language Serves a Country Better

			Frequency	Percent
Strongly agree			215	23.1
Agree			285	30.6
Disagree			263	28.3
Strongly disagree			145	15.6
		*	22	2.4
	TOTAL		930	100.0
Valid cases	908	*Missing cases		22

The picture that emerges from a consideration of the individual universities also represents a mixed response. In both white English-speaking universities, the Afrikaans speaking University of Stellenbosch and the University of the Western Cape, a slightly higher number of respondents disagreed with the notion that the national interests of the country would be better served by one official language, and this was followed by a slightly lower number of those who agreed with that statement. At the University of Pretoria, the University of Durban-Westville and the University of Zululand, a higher number of students agreed with the statement followed by a slightly lower number of those who disagreed with the statement.

The only university where a higher number of respondents not only "agreed" (31%) but also "strongly agreed" (29%) with the statement is the University of the North. At the opposite end of the statistical pole is the University of Fort Hare where a higher number of respondents not only "disagreed" (28%) but also "strongly disagreed" (23%) with the statement that national interests would be better served by one official language.

The responses to the question of one official language became clearer once a particular language was proposed as an official language. If there was some ambivalence to the idea that the national interests of the country would best be served by one language, any semblance of doubt suddenly disappeared when English was proposed as that official language.

In response to the question whether they were for or against English as the only official language, the combined results showed that more respondents were not just "for" (29%) but "definitely for" (34%) English as the only official language; these values added up to a total rating of 63% for English as the only official language (Table 10.3). That same pattern of responses was evident at the three black universities, the Colored University of the Western Cape, the Indian University of Durban-Westville, the University of the Witwatersrand and the University of Pretoria.

At the University of Stellenbosch more respondents (40%) were against and fewer (25%) were "for" English as the only official language. At the University of Cape Town an equal number of respondents (27%) were not only "against" but "definitely against" (27%) English as the only official language. These two universities were, therefore, the only exceptions to the general pattern of agreement about English as the only official language. That exception underscores the general rule that English emerged in the survey as the only language that qualified as the official language of the new South Africa.

Table 10.3   For or Against English as the Only Official Language

		Frequency	Percent
Definitely for		312	33.5
For		272	29.2
Against		213	22.9
Definitely against		114	12.3
	*	19	2.0
	TOTAL	930	100.0
Valid cases	911	*Missing cases	19

But if English became the only official language in the new South Africa, would that necessarily translate into a demotion of the other languages? The answer to that question in the combined results showed that a higher number of respondents said "no" (42%) but a significant number said "yes" (31%) the recognition of English as the only official language would mean a demotion to the language of each ethnic group (Table 10.4).

Table 10.4   Other Languages would Be Demoted by English as the Only
               Official Language

			Frequency	Percent
Definitely yes			146	15.7
Yes			284	30.5
No			393	42.3
Definitely no			82	8.8
		*	25	2.7
	TOTAL		930	100.0

Valid cases	905	*Missing cases	25

The sole exception was the University of Pretoria which had an almost equal
number of those who said "yes" (37%) and those who said "no" (36%). These
responses may be an indication that there were some strong feelings in the
Afrikaans-speaking university about the Afrikaans language being ranked second
to English, even though the university had declared to be not only "for" but also
"definitely for" English as the only official language. The point needs to be
emphasized that for an Afrikaans-speaking university to be "definitely for"
English as the only official language, when in fact the status of official languages
was shared by both English and Afrikaans, does indicate quite poignantly the
extent to which different ethnic and racial groups are prepared to go to have one
official language in the new South Africa.

To recognize one language, in this case English, as the only official language does
not mean that the different languages should not have the legal right to exist.
Hence the respondents, in the combined results of the survey, were not only "to
an appreciable extent" (27%) but also "very much" (52%) in support of "the right

112

of different racial and ethnic groups to preserve and maintain their own languages"
(Table 10.5). A majority of 79% of the respondents supported the right of other
languages to exist. This pattern of responses in support of different languages to
exist in their own right was repeated in all the different universities without
exception.

Table 10.5   Support for the Right of Different Languages to Exist

			Frequency	Percent
Very much			482	51.8
To an appreciable extent			253	27.2
To some extent			146	15.7
Not at all			24	2.6
		*	25	2.7
	TOTAL		930	100.0
Valid cases	905	*Missing cases		25

Since there are eleven official languages recognized constitutionally in South Africa
and, given the strength of ethnic an racial identities, it   may have to take the
collective will of the people, in the form of a national referendum, to decide finally
on the question of whether English should be the only official language in South
Africa.

In the study, a higher number of respondents were "for" (41%) and a lower
number "definitely for" (26%) the idea of a national referendum to decide on this
question. The idea of a national referendum received a high rating of 68% (Table
10.6).

Individual universities followed the same pattern of responses with the exception of the University of Fort Hare where the support for the idea was also there but not as pronounced as in other universities. At this university a smaller number of respondents were "for" (35%) and an even smaller number were against (26%) the holding of a referendum.

Table 10.6   For or Against a National Referendum on English

	Frequency	Percent
Definitely for	243	26.1
For	385	41.4
Against	192	20.6
Definitely against	89	9.6
*	21	2.3
TOTAL	930	100.0

Valid cases	909	*Missing cases	21

At any rate, if the referendum did take place and English was endorsed by the majority of South Africans as the only official language, would that national decision be accepted or rejected? In the combined results of the study, a significant number of respondents said they would not only accept (46%) but also definitely accept (26%) the national decision. The majority for the idea of acceptance was 72% (Table 10.7).

Table 10.7   Would Respondents Accept or Reject Endorsement of English?

		Frequency	Percent
Definitely accept		243	26.1
Accept		425	45.7
Reject		181	19.5
Definitely reject		59	6.3
	*	22	2.4
	TOTAL	930	100.0
Valid cases	908	*Missing cases	22

The individual universities responded similarly, except for the University of Fort Hare and the University of Zululand which had a slightly different pattern of responses. In both these universities a higher number of respondents declared that they would support the national decision but differed with the rest of the other universities in that they had some opposition to the idea of accepting a national decision on English as the only official language. But this opposition is offset by the higher number of those who were prepared to support the outcome of a referendum.

11

NATIONAL ANTHEM

South Africa has the international distinction of not only having eleven official languages but also two national anthems. The first is NKOSI SIKELEL'IAFRIKA/MORENA BOLOKA SECHABA SA HESO which is associated with the former national liberation movement and the second is DIE STEM, the national anthem when the Afrikaners were ruling the country. The question was, To what extent were the respondents in favor of or against the existence of two national anthems?

In the combined results of the study, the common denominator was that the respondents were either "moderately in favor" (36%) or "strongly in favor" (25%) of the existence of two national anthems (Table 11.1).

This pattern is only repeated in the individual universities at the University of Zululand, the University of the North and the University of Pretoria.

At the University of the Witwatersrand, the University of Fort Hare, the University of the Western Cape and the University of Durban-Westville, a higher number of respondents were also "moderately in favor" but this number was followed by a lower but significant number of those who were "strongly against" the existence of two national anthems.

Table 11.1   In Favor or Against Two National Anthems in South Africa

	Frequency	Percent
Strongly in favor	232	24.9
Moderately in favor	330	35.5
Moderately against	128	13.8
Strongly against	222	23.9
*	18	1.9
TOTAL	930	100.0

Valid cases	912	*Missing cases	18

At the University of Cape Town, the majority of respondents (58%) were "strongly against" the existence of two anthems. At the University of Stellenbosch, a small number (30%) were "moderately in favor" but a slightly higher number (35%) were "strongly against" the existence of two national anthems.

The idea that the two anthems might have to be amalgamated has been discussed in South Africa. The views about this matter according to the study indicate that, in the combined results, the respondents were either "moderately in favor" (34%) or "strongly in favor" (25%) of one amalgamated national anthem which combines parts from both the existing ones (Table 11.2).

Four universities considered separately followed a similar pattern of responses: the University of the Witwatersrand, the University of the Western Cape, the University of Zululand and the University of the North.

118

Table 11.2   In Favor or Against One Amalgamated National Anthem

		Frequency	Percent
Strongly in favor		236	25.4
Moderately in favor		313	33.7
Moderately against		142	15.3
Strongly against		214	23.0
	*	25	2.7
	TOTAL	930	100.0
Valid cases	905	*Missing cases	25

At the University of Fort Hare, the University of Durban-Westville and the University of Pretoria, a higher number of respondents were "moderately in favor" and a lower but significant number was "strongly against" an amalgamated national anthem. The University of Stellenbosch had an equal number of respondents (25%) who were "moderately in favor", "moderately against" and "strongly against." The only clear opposition to an amalgamated national anthem was at the University of Cape Town where 44% were "strongly against" and 22% "moderately against."

The general consensus was "moderately in favor" of an amalgamated national anthem.

119

12

LEADERS

Unquestionably, from the 1980's the apartheid regime faced increasing pressure both internally and externally to abandon the apartheid system. When it finally became apparent to the white power structure that white supremacy was about to end, the central question was whether president F.W. de Klerk would be prepared to preside over the demise of the system. Could he persuade his people that the time had come to abandon the Afrikaner laager and begin the negotiation process for the new South Africa?

The question that was raised in the survey was whether F.W. de Klerk, in terms of this leadership of the Nationalist Party, played a major role in persuading the white electorate to abandon the apartheid system. In the combined results, the majority of the respondents (61%) agreed with the statement that F.W. de Klerk played a major role in convincing the white electorate to give up apartheid and turn to negotiations for a new South Africa (Table 12.1).

That pattern of collective responses was repeated in the individual universities with the exception of the University of Cape Town where a higher number of respondents (44%) disagreed and a lower number (34%) agreed that de Klerk had played a major role in swaying the white electorate towards the negotiation process.

121

Table 12.1   F.W. de Klerk Persuaded White Electorate to Abandon Apartheid

			Frequency	Percent
Agree			567	61.0
Uncertain			193	20.8
Disagree			152	16.3
		*	18	1.9
	TOTAL		930	100.0
Valid cases	912		*Missing cases	18

At the University of Fort Hare, the respondents were equally divided between those who agreed (33%) that de Klerk had played a major role and those who were "uncertain" (33%) about that role. The highest numbers of those who agreed that de Klerk had played a major role were registered at the University of Pretoria (80%) and the University of Stellenbosch (75%).

It was one thing for de Klerk to persuade the predominantly Afrikaner whites to desert the apartheid bandwagon and another thing to convince them to accept change that would enable blacks to share power with whites and usher in an era of inevitable black political power. The question was whether de Klerk had played a major role in winning over his followers to the idea of change.

The majority of respondents (63%) in the combined results agreed that de Klerk had played an important role in persuading the white electorate to accept change (Table 12.2). The only exception to this collective response was at the University of Cape Town where a slightly higher number of respondents (39%) disagreed and a slightly lower number (37%) agreed with the statement that de Klerk had played a major role in persuading the white electorate to accept change.

122

Table 12.2   F.W. de Klerk Persuaded White Electorate to Accept Change

			Frequency	Percent
Agree			584	62.8
Uncertain			191	20.5
Disagree			134	14.4
		*	21	2.3
	TOTAL		930	100.0
Valid cases	909		*Missing cases	21

Nelson Mandela received the highest rating (88%) for his major contribution to the struggle for freedom in South Africa (Table 12.3). Five universities: the University of Cape Town, the University of the Witwatersrand, the University of the Western Cape, the University of Durban-Westville, and the University of the North gave him a rating of over 90%. The University of Fort Hare and the University of Zululand gave him a rating of over 80%; the University of Stellenbosch and the University of Pretoria gave him a rating of 75% and over. By any standard of measurement, these were very high and very impressive ratings.

These high ratings, however, dropped drastically when president Mandela's role after the non-racial elections of April 1994 was evaluated. Asked whether Nelson Mandela had done much, since his inauguration as president, to restore confidence in democracy in South Africa, the majority of respondents (65%), for the whole sample, agreed that he had (Table 12.4). But, compared to the high rating he received for his overall contribution to the struggle for freedom, this second rating constitutes a drop of 23%.

Table 12.3   N. Mandela Made a Major Contribution to Struggle for Freedom

		Frequency	Percent
Agree		816	87.7
Uncertain		64	6.9
Disagree		32	3.4
	*	18	1.9
	TOTAL	930	100.0
Valid cases	912	*Missing cases	18

In the case of individual universities, Nelson Mandela received his highest rating (81%) from the University of the Western Cape. Three universities: the University of Cape Town, the University of the Witwatersrand and the University of the North gave Mandela a rating of over 70%. The University of Zululand gave him 60% and the University of Pretoria, the University of Stellenbosch and the University of Durban-Westville gave him a rating of just over 50%. The lowest rating came from the University of Fort Hare where he received only 47% for his contribution in restoring confidence in democracy in South Africa. This lowest rating was probably because the rival political organization, the PAC, had strong support at this institution.

Table 12.4   Mandela Restored Confidence in Democracy in South Africa

			Frequency	Percent
Agree			606	65.2
Uncertain			208	22.4
Disagree			95	10.2
		*	21	2.3
	TOTAL		930	100.0
Valid cases	909		*Missing cases	21

The positions taken respectively by the University of Pretoria, the University of Stellenbosch and Durban-Westville could easily be interpreted as reflections of ethnic concerns or fear of black domination on the part of the Indian and Afrikaner minorities, but, the same could not be said of the University of Fort Hare, a black university, where the majority of students are Xhosa-speaking, the same ethnic group as Mandela. There is clearly some concern on the part of respondents that Mandela's contribution to the restoration of confidence in democracy does not compare favorably with his major contribution to the struggle for freedom.

If Mandela was not so highly rated in his presidential role to restore confidence in democracy, the question was whether the respondents agreed or disagreed that president Nelson Mandela was the social glue that kept blacks and whites together in South Africa. The response to that question, in the combined results, indicates that a high number (70%) (Table 12.5) of respondents believed the president was in fact the social glue that kept the two historically antagonistic segments of the population together.

This pattern of responses was repeated in all the individual universities, with the highest rating (82%) coming from the University of the North and the lowest (56%) from the University of Fort Hare. From these ratings, it can be inferred that racial harmony in South Africa can be largely attributed to the stabilizing presence of Nelson Mandela. And so the question arises, What kind of stability can be expected after Mandela? In other words, to what extent were the respondents apprehensive about the future stability of South Africa after Mandela?

Table 12.5   Mandela is the Social Glue that Kept Whites & Blacks Together

		Frequency	Percent
Agree		649	69.8
Uncertain		210	22.6
Disagree		54	5.8
*		17	1.8
	TOTAL	930	100.0

Valid cases	913	*Missing cases	17

The sample results indicate that there was some concern about the future stability of South Africa after Mandela, ranging from higher numbers relating to slight and moderate apprehension and lower numbers relating to those who were very much apprehensive; 50% were either moderately or very apprehensive (Table 12.6).

Table 12.6   Apprehension About the Future after Mandela

	Frequency	Percent
Not at all apprehensive	117	12.6
Slightly apprehensive	324	34.8
Moderately apprehensive	252	27.1
Very much apprehensive	212	22.8
*	25	2.7
TOTAL	930	100.0

Valid cases	905	*Missing cases	25

This pattern of ratings is repeated at the University of the Witwatersrand, the University of the Western Cape, the University of the North and the University of Fort Hare. At the University of Zululand respondents were "slightly apprehensive" (36%) and "very much apprehensive" (22%). Also at the University of Stellenbosch a number of students were "slightly apprehensive" (40%) followed by the category of those who were "very much apprehensive" (25%). At the University of Durban-Westville more respondents were "moderately apprehensive" (39%) than those who were "slightly apprehensive" (29%). At the University of Cape Town more respondents were "moderately apprehensive" (41%) than those who were "slightly apprehensive" (29%). The only university where more respondents were "very much apprehensive" (29%) followed by those who were "slightly apprehensive" (28%) was the University of Pretoria.

The only clear common denominator, at the level of individual universities, was that more universities had respondents who were slightly apprehensive (six) than those who were moderately apprehensive (two). Only one university had more respondents who were very much apprehensive about the future after Mandela.

PART II

THE OPEN QUESTION

13

RESPONSES

Overview

The open question on power sharing was meant to give the respondents the opportunity to state their views freely, without the constraints and limitations imposed by the structured questions. The respondents were specifically asked to elaborate on the advantages and/or disadvantages of power sharing which had become the corner stone of the GNU in the new South Africa. Their responses reflected individual opinions and were expressed in various ways but in the final analysis they had common elements which could be grouped into specific major themes.

The views relating to the advantages of power sharing could be grouped into four broad categories:

1. Reconciliation and Peace
2. Representation and Non Domination
3. Experience and Development
4. Transition and Continuity

Opinions spelling out the disadvantages of power sharing could also be reduced to four major categories:

1. Neocolonialism
2. Destabilization
3. Hegemony
4. Power, Privilege and Poverty

In the grouping and analysis of responses, each of the nine universities covered in the study had to be treated separately to get a sense of the preponderance of views in a particular university and the general pattern of preferences associated with that institution. This meant that, in focusing on individual institutions, there would be an inevitable repetition of similar responses even though the depth and sophistication of those responses would differ from institution to institution. Also, not all major categories relating to the advantages and disadvantages of power sharing were addressed in the responses from individual universities.

THE UNIVERSITY OF THE NORTH

Advantages of Power Sharing

Reconciliation and Peace

At the University of the North many respondents viewed power sharing as an advantage because in the final analysis it helped to promote reconciliation and peace. They pointed out that through power sharing there would be better understanding, shared responsibility, tolerance of each others' views, a sense of security on the part of minority groups, promotion of good will, activation of trust, a feeling of complete citizenship and a sense of general satisfaction. Working closely and interacting with one's opponents was viewed as a major advantage. As one respondent put it:

"A nearby or an enemy at a close range is easy to defeat or deal with than a hidden or far away one."

A similar view was stated by one respondent who expressed hope for the future because of power sharing:

"If power is shared by political parties political differences can easily be resolved....If power is shared I have hope for peace and stability."
Other views emphasized the advantages of power sharing for those political parties involved in the process:

"The political parties are exposed in a scenario of political tolerance, understanding and debating issues in good faith."

And along the same lines another respondent stated that "all political parties and all groups of different kinds of people are accommodated to participate in South African activities."

On the question of peace specifically, it was pointed out by one respondent that "power sharing brought peace and harmony; if it was one party the other parties outside government would resort to violence to overthrow the existing government."

In a racially polarized country like South Africa, power sharing is viewed by one respondent as being necessary because "it keeps the Blacks and white population together particularly in the first year(s) of the newly born nonracial democratic South Africa."

Another respondent went further than the question of peace and pointed out that power sharing is "a better basis for democracy than outright majority rule so it needs to be a permanent feature of the South African political structure." Along the same lines, one respondent pointed out that power sharing "would prevent a particular political party to assume too much power that could possibly result in dictatorship."

The relationship of power sharing to peace is particularly emphasized by respondents who saw it as "a means of stopping civil war" and of reducing "political violence and political intimidation." In terms of race relations, a one party type of government "would not have the support of the whites especially in the military."

From the point of view of black people, "power sharing is a sign of our willingness to forgive and forget." This demonstration of the willingness of the black majority to forgive and forget was necessary because "white people particularly were very apprehensive and very uncomfortable with the idea of being suddenly governed by a black majority government." Furthermore, power sharing is an advantage in a country that is "dominated by ethical and racial divisions." The sharing of political power "helps one to identify with the nation irrespective of his racial background." In a racially and ethnically divided society, it is the basis for understanding and peace because if power "is 'rationally' distributed among all the people, the result is likely to be that of understanding....because there will be transparency in everything and this could lead to a nonviolent, peaceful South Africa."

Representation and Non Domination

One of the major arguments of the advocates of the apartheid system related to the notion of the prevention of the domination of one racial group by another. Whites, who were in fact dominating blacks, were supposed to develop along their own lines and blacks, who were divided further along ethnic lines by their white rulers, were required to pursue their own development in their own ethnic mini states. In the era of apartheid, whites were determined to maintain white supremacy and blacks pursued every means at their disposal to try to bring it down. Blacks and whites were polarized along racial lines and this, in essence, constituted the South African conflict. But after the dismantling of the apartheid system, power sharing became an important element of the Government of National Unity.

Many respondents who participated in the study indicated that it was because of the representation of the different parties in the GNU that conflict was eliminated. As respondents representing this perspective stated:

"Power sharing eliminated war...No other party dominates the others."
"....Racial groups have an opportunity to be represented."
"The only advantage of power sharing is to make every political party to participate in the decisions made during parliamentary gatherings."

Participation in the decision making process by minority parties was considered to be an important matter because minority parties were seen to be in constant fear of domination. Participation was also viewed to be good, not just for the political parties, but for the country as a whole because South Africa "is made up of numbers of nationalities which all need recognition and power of their own."

Power sharing "gives all the people in South Africa to say their views in parliament through their parties." Power sharing is necessary in South Africa to avoid a "situation of dictatorship." It can "to some extent, ensure cooperation among the leading politicians in the government." Power sharing is "most advantageous due to the fact that South Africa is a multicultural and heterogeneous country....Hence the need for individual party's representation in the post-apartheid government. This can clear the differences between parties and coerce them into a common, unanimous and unified government representing the whole society."

It is the overall impact of power sharing on the various constituents in the country, in terms of promoting the spirit of tolerance, that makes power sharing so important. As one respondent put it:

" Even the voice of the minority representatives is taken into serious consideration. As long as the leaders are comfortable with leaders of opposing parties, the followers are usually also tolerant to the opposing groups."

Experience and Development

It was a basic tenet of the apartheid system that it would be to the greater benefit of the country if whites and blacks developed along separate lines. However, after the demise of the apartheid regime and the introduction of power sharing, the emphasis shifted to cooperation and collaboration for the greater good of the country.

It was in that same light of cooperation and tolerance that many respondents saw the advantages of power sharing in the new South Africa. From this perspective power sharing "leads to the 'closest and fullest' allowance of different groups, parties, cultures - as a result it enhances development of a country politically and economically to maintain stability." And a country that is stable and developing is in a better position "to woo foreign investment."

The important point about development as emphasized by the respondents is that political cooperation and economic growth go hand in hand and would impact positively on the country: "Economic growth and political accommodation would be beneficial to South Africa." In the words of another respondent, "power sharing for nation building, reconciliation and development is very essential."

One of the biggest problems inherited from the apartheid era is the enormous gap between the haves and haves-not in South Africa. This problem, in the view of one respondent, can be surmounted because of the role of power sharing which "will bridge the socio-economic gap between the rich and the poor in our community." As a result of political power sharing there would be a better distribution of wealth and "everyone in the country will be able to have a share of the wealth of his own country."

The lack of experience on the part of black leaders is seen by one respondent as one of the reasons why power sharing is so important to the country. Power sharing from this perspective is particularly advantageous to blacks because "blacks have never been in power so it is advisable for them to share power with whites because the whites know what is taking place in the government, how they organize things in the government; they know more about means of improving the country on economical basis and on technological advancement. The majority of them are educated and civilized." Therefore, in the view of another respondent, "some parties who have the knowledge of everything should help i.e. come up with ideas and use their experience on how to govern, which is advantageous to the people...."

Transition and Continuity

Historically, under white domination, South Africa evolved as a country without a culture of democracy. During the apartheid period, blacks were excluded from participating in the political process by law. Through the power sharing arrangement the minority parties, including the former white ruling party, the Nationalist Party, were allowed to participate in the GNU to effect a smooth and stable transition from dictatorship to democracy.

One respondent conceded that power sharing was necessary for a stable transition but added that "I will however not recommend power sharing to be entrenched in the final constitution after this nursing/healing period of transition." From this perspective power sharing is viewed simply as a temporary measure to usher in the era of a stable democracy.

Power sharing was not only necessary as an inclusive tool that would enable the former rulers to participate in the democratic process, but it would help the new leaders to do the right thing because "in the absence of power sharing, the government of the day will tend to misuse power to further its own interest." Therefore, from this perspective, the meeting of the old and the new order in the context of power sharing would ensure continuity in the knowledge and expertise required to govern the country.

Disadvantages of Power Sharing

Neocolonialism

On the negative, the concept of power sharing was critically viewed and even rejected outright by a number of respondents.

South Africa is undoubtedly the most advanced capitalist country in Africa and as such has strong ties with other capitalist countries, most notably Britain, France, Germany, Japan and the United States. The white minority groups in South Africa had and still have strong and firm relationships with the capitalist world and it is because of these continuing bonds that one respondent argued that "unfortunately the powerful minority will remain powerful for ever because they are collaborating and enjoy privileges from the most powerful supremacist U.S.A."

Therefore from the perspective of the capitalist nature of the country and its strong links with the capitalist world, many respondents saw the old order in South Africa remaining powerful and perpetuating neocolonial relationships. Apartheid as a dominant political force may have been dismantled but it continues in neocolonial terms because power sharing "is used as a tool to promote and maintain apartheid under cover." In the words of another respondent "power sharing is limited in South Africa because most of the Blacks are still serving hounds of the apartheid regime." Blacks may now be holding the reins of political power but the reality is that "power sharing brings the feeling of being in office and not in power or government."

Destabilization

Through power sharing the black majority government may take long to realize its objectives because "other political leaders can abuse their powers" in attempts to destabilize the government. And, apart from the question of abuse of power, "decisions can take longer to be made because of the involvement of many people with different opinions."

Power sharing is therefore seen to be weakening instead of strengthening the government. For the government to be strong and effective it cannot do so within the framework of power sharing. Power sharing should be used as a temporary measure only: "Five years is appropriate and beyond that the winner must take all....Gone are the days of boereskap."

Power sharing "legitimizes reactionary forces." And, therefore, "the ruling party cannot carry out its policies without hindrance." Power sharing is "a stumbling block for a government when it wants to take [a] firm stance on some national issues...." and this is due to the fact that "smaller parties sometimes are bent to sabotage the whole process coming with the leading political parties in that

140

government." The end result is that "the majority party faces too much criticism than others."

In short, in the views of a number of respondents, power sharing may be good in theory but in practice it can be a major obstacle. As one respondent summarized this point of view:

"The concept is good in principle but it led to the delay of implementation of the policy of the majority political party, especially to address and fulfill the promises they made to their supporters and on the same breath [the] white minority still wants to frustrate the program of the government and so undermine the African leadership."

Hegemony

Power sharing may be important because political parties share ideas and concerns but, on the negative side, such a political arrangement is problematic because "every political party would like to be the leading party even if it knows that it does not deserve to be the leader." The natural tendency is for political parties to take leadership positions and to dominate others, thus making power sharing problematic. As one respondent bluntly put it: "People cannot share power for obvious reasons. There has to be a boss everywhere, even animals have a tendency to domination. The majority party has to be the government of the day."

The only problem in the case of South Africa is that the majority party may not have many black people who are knowledgeable and experienced enough to run the government efficiently. Therefore, as one respondent pointed out, "whites will want to be dominant because they know much. Blacks have been long deprived privileges of education and knowledge and that is why they will not contribute much if they are alone in the government." This means that they cannot "express their potentiality of how much they know." To summarize, from the point of view of these respondents, blacks in the majority party may be in office but they do not really have the power of real leaders because of their lack of governmental knowledge which was always monopolized by whites.

In the final analysis power sharing may actually be more mythical than real. As one respondent put it with regard to the role of whites in government:

"I am not convinced that really politicians can share power to a satisfactory degree. What is perceived in the history of mankind is that there will be those who are influential in the running of the country. As such their views and proposals will always take the lead in the government."

Power, Privilege and Poverty

A recurring theme in a number of responses is that politicians share power to realize their political ambitions and not necessarily to use their power base to help the needy. In the view of one respondent "Power sharing may only concentrate on those holding power but forgetting who made it possible for it to exist."

The majority party, the ANC, raised high hopes and expectations on the part of blacks that it would deal effectively with their state of poverty. However, once in office, "the government seemed much to be concerned with white fears than addressing the needs of the black majority." Therefore, power sharing is "to the disadvantage of the indigenous Africans. Power sharing favors whites who own the means of production."

The wide economic gap between whites and blacks would not be bridged because "the whites would continue to practice capitalism." One of the reasons black leaders find it so difficult to deal effectively with the level of poverty affecting

142

blacks is that "though black people would have had political power, that power would not have been supplemented by economic power, since the majority of the economic power is centered in white hands...."

The ruling party should normally bear the blame and take full responsibility for failing to fulfill its election promises but, as one respondent observed, due to power sharing, "it is not easy to identify as to whether the party I voted for is really delivering the goods or not."

Some respondents also made a passing reference to power sharing in relation to the combined national anthems, one representing the old apartheid regime and the other the liberation movement. One respondent described the combined national anthem as "comprising of two different songs which is marked by totally different and contradictory histories of the Boers and Blacks." Another respondent made the remark that "the national anthem must also be truly African i.e. without Die Stem as its component part."

The respondents at the University of the North viewed power sharing as having both good and bad points. On the whole, the concept was seen as a necessary, albeit temporary, arrangement that must eventually be done away with. As one respondent put it: "I will however not recommend power sharing to be entrenched in the final constitution after this nursing/healing period of transition."

THE UNIVERSITY OF DURBAN-WESTVILLE

The respondents at the University of Durban-Westville were fewer in numbers, compared to the University of the North, but their comments on the contribution of power sharing to reconciliation and peace were on the same lines.

Advantages of Power Sharing

Reconciliation and Peace

Respondents at the University of Durban-Westville regarded power sharing as important because "it will bring about reconciliation, peace and stability." It is seen as an ideal system for "peace and harmony" and involves "collaborative governance" where all parties "learn to tolerate each other."

Representation and Non Domination

Power sharing provides for "peace of mind concerning political rule." It allows "equal representation for all races and ethnic groups unlike majority rule.

Transition and Continuity

Power sharing is important during the transitional period because "South Africa has made a radical change from apartheid to democracy." It also "helps people feel that they do have representation in the GNU."

At the point of transition blacks had no alternative but "to succumb to a system of powers", but this must be viewed as a temporary measure in order to make the regime "get used to the situation of not being in power." And as soon as " the latter aim has been achieved the power of Black people only and exclusively will make its way."

Disadvantages of Power Sharing

Destabilization

Power sharing, overall, has a destabilizing effect because it "leads to negotiation and inevitably to parties compromising their positions on certain issues to ensure harmony in the government."

One respondent summarized the obstacles of power sharing to the new regime in these words:

> i, The leading party might experience problems that are caused by the
> members of other parties intentionally, in order to discredit it.
> ii, Members of the leading majority party might impose their views and
> crash the minority.
> iii, Conflicts tend to arise in parliament and it becomes hard to reach
> consensus, and as a result, the government might become stagnant and fail
> to deliver to the people.

146

Poverty, Power and Privilege

Power sharing was seen by one respondent as an obstacle to the upward mobility of the historically disadvantaged majority because "it gives people who have been in power before more power and benefits at the expense of people who have been at a disadvantage for their whole lives." Furthermore, as applied, power sharing "does not include power sharing in terms of wealth minerals etc."

Another respondent commented on the effects of power sharing on the Indian minority:

"From my experiences I have found that the 'man in the street' has a strange concept of the new S.A. They believe that since we have a new (sic), automatically it implies a black government where only the black language and culture is recognized...."

With regard to the new national anthem, the same respondent stated: "I also believe that the anthem Nkosi Sikelele iAfrika represents only the black population whereas Die Stem represents the white population. For unity and democracy and equality for all, I believe that a new anthem should be written - one that represents South Africa and one that can be sung in any language."

UNIVERSITY OF ZULULAND

Responses to the open question at the University of Zululand were many. However, the majority of them were similar in content and imparted no new information. Therefore, to avoid unnecessary repetition, only a representative sample of these responses is cited.

Advantages of Power Sharing

Reconciliation and Peace

At the University of Zululand, power sharing was viewed as a positive step provided "it is done fairly and without bias." One respondent expressed a strong belief in power sharing because "it brings everybody together politically and economically." It was also seen as leading to better understanding because "people learn more about each other, especially culturally." Another respondent visualized power sharing as playing an important role in race relations and stated that "if power sharing could be a permanent feature of S.A. we can all live in a harmonious way." The transient nature of power sharing was emphasized by a respondent who argued that the ideal is "majority rule within a democratic system." If that ideal is realized, and "if this could be guaranteed with no false promises made to the electorate then power sharing can be ended."

Ultimately, for those who were historically excluded from governance, power sharing is seen as restoring the sense of belonging to the country. In the words of one respondent, power sharing "makes one to feel a complete citizen of the country because he or she knows that he or she has a word in the governing of the country."

Representation and Non Domination

The survival of democracy is seen by one respondent as dependent on power sharing. According to this respondent power sharing is "the cornerstone of democracy" and, therefore, to "maintain democracy in our country, the people.... should share the power that may be." But another argued that there is an inherent danger in power sharing due to the role of minority parties. Representation is built into the system of power sharing and "minority groupings are at least assured of their interest being attended to but this may be dangerous in that they may push for unreasonable demands under this concept."

Experience and Development

Power sharing is seen as contributing to development because it "ensures maximum productivity since there is fair distribution of wealth." Team work on the part of political groups involved in power sharing "leads to commitment of them all to the development of the country's welfare and stability."

Transition and Continuity

Continuity in governance is underlined by one respondent who focused on the lack of experience on the part of blacks and maintained that "power sharing is all right for South Africa because blacks cannot rule alone. They need a white man."

150

Disadvantages of Power Sharing

Destabilization

The disadvantage of power sharing, according to one respondent, is that it "creates a lot of conflicts when a major decision has to be made. All parties must be consulted." The same point regarding destabilization of the process of governance is made by one respondent who points out that "others have called the power sharing government "a government of national crisis" because since it began there has been no agreement reached." The question of destabilization is also addressed by one respondent who stated that " I am strongly against power sharing as it destabilizes the government of the day."

Hegemony

A number of respondents saw hegemonic tendencies as one of the problems of power sharing. In the view of one respondent, who was apparently making a veiled reference to the dominant role of the ANC, "there is no power share [sic] in the parliament; only the needs of one organization being served." Another respondent pointed out that power sharing "makes it difficult for voters to determine the ability of those in power...." In other words, it is not easy to ascertain "whether they are able to run the country successfully." The same respondent then proceeded to say that "I would therefore prefer that in future the party that wins and gets the majority vote, should govern the country." A similar point is made by another respondent who indicated that "power struggle becomes a major block of progress as all political parties strive for leadership than for development of their country."

Power, Privilege and Poverty

The relatively more privileged life of white South Africans, in comparison to the poor one of black South African, comes under severe criticism by one respondent who said that "whites are still occupying better positions....[B]lacks are the majority in South Africa but they are occupying 13% of the land; if you go to the townships the infrastructure is not acceptable and living conditions are just not suitable for human beings. Its like a zoo that is not taken care of."

Harping on the same theme of inequities between whites and blacks, another respondent asked: "How can there be power sharing where there is no equal economic status?" A pointed criticism is directed at the power elite structure as a whole by one respondent who had reservations about power sharing because, in his words, " I have not yet seen S.A. sharing power in its fullest...people in the top are preaching the gospel of this power sharing yet people in the grassroots level have nothing to share with them."

Along the same lines of economic disparity, one respondent pointed out that the disadvantage of power sharing is that "some people are remaining poor." Another poured ridicule on the concept of power sharing because "people in Parliament enjoy fat cheques and they never think about the man in the street."

UNIVERSITY OF THE WESTERN CAPE

Advantages of Power Sharing

Reconciliation and Peace

Power sharing is rated highly by one respondent at the University of the Western Cape who asserts that "power sharing in South Africa promotes a spirit of equality, reconciliation, stability and a just society." In the same vein, another respondent states that "reconciliation is possible because most parties share ideas and see each other as people to argue with instead of seeing each other as enemies." Again, as another put it, "power sharing has been the key to peace and positive future relations in South Africa."

This line of thinking, which extols the virtues of power sharing, is challenged by other respondents who emphasize the democratic right of the majority to rule. As one expressed it, "of course power sharing is good but it must not be the central issue of this country. There were people who were deprived. They must be given their right to rule." The same point is strongly underscored by one respondent who states that "power sharing is necessary for the transformation or transference of power, but it must be limited to some or agreed upon period....[I]t must not be prolonged beyond the period agreed upon by the multiparty conference." The

153

same respondent further points out that "the other parties who constitute a minority within the government of National Unity are responsible for shifting the implementation of the transformation process. Therefore majority rule is the answer to the problems of South Africa."

The respondents, therefore, generally agree that, in the words of one of them, "power sharing can contribute to the rebuilding of this shattered country of ours from the ashes of apartheid. It can contribute to peace, economic growth and even to reconciliation." But, as the same respondent points out, "it is ironic because in most cases it is Black people who are bending over backwards to reconcile white people who are not honest, especially the older ones. White youth is better."

This negative element relating to the older generation of whites notwithstanding, one respondent states that "we are truly a 'rainbow nation', and because of this power sharing is important and advantageous....with power sharing different parties would feel they have a role to play in this newly developing democracy in our country."

Representation and Non Domination

In South Africa, being a multiethnic and multiracial society, the question of minority representation is a major issue which is addressed by one respondent who states that power sharing "protects minorities who would otherwise have no access to political power - in terms of race and ethnicity." This respondent, however, projects a different picture of a new South Africa that should not be preoccupied with issues of race and ethnicity and states: "Personally, I would like to see the people of South Africa start to identify with each other on the basis of their "South Africanism" and put an end to all the myriads of cleavages in terms of ethnicity - however idealistic this may seem." In the final analysis, power sharing, in the view of another correspondent, "prevents domination of one party

154

(group) over another, allows people to voice their opinion because they are represented in government" and "will prevent dictatorship as had happened in so many states in Africa."

But the question of non domination is not the major issue from the perspective of respondents who emphasize the right of the historically oppressed majority to exercise power. One of them elaborated on this question:

> If a people have been oppressed like the black South Africans, power sharing will not correct the imbalances which have been existent in this particular society. Majority rule in this case is the correct approach to address the imbalances which have been prevalent. Power sharing is like attaining political office and not attaining political power.

Disadvantages of Power Sharing

Neocolonialism

Power sharing is viewed by one respondent as a "sellout position" despite the fact that "it avoided civil war." This particular respondent argues that the "struggle is not over....because South Africans are on the receiving end." Therefore, "South Africa needs a radical way of transformation, not through concessions, nor compromises at the expense of the down trodden mass." Furthermore, in terms of the position of the historically disadvantaged group, power sharing was seen to be more of a disadvantage because it meant that "social change was going to be very slow. It had a negative connotation."

The idea that power sharing was seen to be more of a disadvantage to blacks meant that whites in South Africa were the main beneficiaries of the new political dispensation. As one respondent observed, "power sharing as a concept in a South

155

African context is to appease only those who were in the government of minority who wanted to cling to power (and) to show their supporters they were still in power." In the view of another, "power sharing will entail addressing white fears rather than dealing with the problem of uplifting those who have been discriminated against i.e. blacks.... So power sharing means white rule in disguise."

Power sharing, therefore, "has compromised majority rule which South African people had been fighting for all the past years." As a result, "no party, whatever the support it enjoys, can implement its political program."

Power, Privilege and Poverty

In the opinion of a number of respondents, the majority of blacks in South Africa do not benefit economically from the sharing of power which they view to be at the political level only. In fact, in one view, "as yet power sharing does not exist. Most of the power, especially economic power, is limited to whites." The disadvantage of power sharing, in another view, is that "Blacks, who are the majority, will be exploited."

The question of white power is stressed further by one respondent who states that:

> [I]n principle, I am not against power sharing as such. But the situation
> here in South Africa is different in the sense that white people still control
> economic power. So the ANC and its allies find themselves trapped within
> this system; that's why noble projects like RDP and Affirmative Action
> have hardly taken off the ground. In a sense the ANC finds itself co-opted
> within the system.

156

In the words of another respondent "power sharing will make more blacks to suffer, in the name of democracy and reconciliation. Power sharing will entail that the rich become rich, (the poor poorer)."

THE UNIVERSITY OF THE WITWATERSRAND

Advantages of Power Sharing

Reconciliation and Peace

The new political dispensation of power sharing is viewed by some respondents at WITS as a progressive and positive philosophy, given the tendency of those in power to be self-centered and selfish. It is seen as a far cry from the apartheid system which restricted absolute control to the white minority. As one respondent put it:

> Power sharing is the surest way to deter power hungry politicians and leaders. Power sharing will keep the new South Africa from becoming like the old.
>
> The principle of sharing is the key issue as opposed to selfishness and self-centeredness. Looking at history and present day world politics, it is clear that the human race tends toward self-protection, self-centeredness and power hungry despotism. The Biblical principle i.e. of sharing, loving one another more than ourselves and lifting others up more than ourselves is the only way to change history and the present. Otherwise, we can

159

expect the nature of human selfishness to perpetuate corrupt and problematic government - a new apartheidism will emerge....

Another respondent reiterated the same ideas and pointed out that "power sharing is positive and necessary especially in a country like South Africa, where decisions along racial lines had become a problem for a long period of time.... a useful mechanism because of its unifying character - most of the South African population is represented." Ethnic minorities would feel at home because "it is the most accommodative system, on which ethnicities can be equally and democratically represented."

The importance of power sharing during the transitional period is emphasized:

Power sharing is definitely appropriate for the transitional period. This ensures that all parties should be responsible for undoing the misdeeds of the past; it also serves to soften the blow of a new government and democracy on those who never wished for a change. As a result, people see the future in more or less the same light.

In the same vein another respondent stated that:

Power sharing does have its advantages in the medium term because, as currently, consensus can be reached on some issues without much hassle, unlike in majoritarian rule where minorities may be completely disregarded, i.e. their will may not be considered - leading to the tyranny of the majority.

According to one respondent, power sharing should not only be seen as something important during the transitional period but also as a necessary evil:

Power sharing in South Africa is something I would describe as necessary but unfortunate. Necessary because we have to avoid violence by Right wing organizations and the IFP. Necessary because the people with financial power remain white and we have to keep them feeling safe and represented, if we are not going to alienate their money.

Unfortunate because it enables the Nationalists and the white capitalists to hold a hand on the lever of power.

Representation and Non Domination

In the view of one respondent, power sharing "prevents any single party from totally dominating the political process, and in so doing, favoring one particular part of the population." Power sharing is, therefore, advantageous because "no one ethnic or political grouping is given 'free reign' over national decision making." On the contrary it "gives black people a chance to get positions of power, not to intimidate or dominate people but to enjoy and participate in aspects of careers and politics that have responsibility and decision making." This is how one respondent summarized the advantages of power sharing to the major contending groups:

Quite simply rule in SA, by either blacks or whites, will be a vehicle for oppressing the other population group. Through power sharing the Afrikaner conservative is reluctantly satisfied, the Zulu nation is appeased and the middle class (white) "semi-liberal" is relieved. However, a divided government, although for a good cause, is nevertheless a weakened government.

Experience and Development

In terms of governmental experience, one respondent underlined the shortcomings of the new leadership in South Africa and pointed out that "our main leaders now, including Mandela, have no idea about running a country - although up to now they have proved capable.... [T]hey need to be assisted by their predecessors to ensure peace and stability."

The same point is reiterated by another respondent who maintained that power sharing " allows those who have never run a country before to learn how to do so. Many political parties were previously liberation movements and have not got a clue about how to govern."

Disadvantages of Power Sharing

Neocolonialism

Power sharing is regarded as a useful concept in the South African context of racial and ethnic politics but, in the view of one respondent, "the concept of reconciliation seems to be one sided." The respondent elaborated further and pointed out that " I really don't believe that most whites are anyway concerned about reconciliation or the issue might be that Blacks are taking it too far - too much forgiving."

If most whites are not interested in reconciliation as some respondents maintain, the question then arises whether some of them can pose serious obstacles to the role of the new government and, if so, in what way. This question is addressed by one respondent:

> To some extent, power sharing is used by some conservatives to block the actual reconstruction and removal of past injustices and imbalances. It

tends to defeat the whole purpose of a new political structure and goal, that is to cure or correct, and also to prevent in future, what has happened in the past.

Power sharing is not what we the majority of South Africans were looking for. The struggle was not for power sharing but for total liberation and majority rule. Instead, power sharing tends to protect too much the interests and privileges of the minority to the detrimental effect of the needs and aspirations of those who have long been disadvantaged and were at the receiving end of the past settler establishment - Apartheid Nationalist Party-led government.

A number of respondents saw power sharing to be antithetical to the concepts of democracy and majority rule:

The concept of democracy under the power sharing type of government loses its weight and significance.... Power sharing is simply to hold democracy at ransom because the will of the majority is not respected.... [T]his concept is a fallacy and it perpetuated white domination. After all, what is political power without economic leverage.

In the view of another respondent it simply comes down to the question of majority rule: "the power should belong to those who get higher votes. By sharing power, opportunists get a share of the 'cake.' This is unacceptable."

The economic plight of blacks becomes a major issue in the view of those respondents who view political power sharing as an obstacle to economic justice. One respondent advanced this viewpoint in uncompromising terms:

Power sharing helps perpetuate racial inequity in S.A. Instead of radical democratization, the government finds itself having to appease beneficiaries of the old order (administrative bureaucracy, military and police hierarchies)! Black people do not gain anything . They have to compromise some of their ideals (the land redistribution program has serious constitutional constraints). The empowerment of blacks, as it inevitably leads to white loss of privileges, gets opposed by the Nationalist Party whose support is indispensable for the work of the Govt. of National Unity. We do not need power sharing in S.A; we need clear majority rule to ensure complete transformation of the country.

Another respondent challenged the idea that power sharing is necessary in racially and ethnically divided societies where minorities need to be protected from the tyranny of the majority:

It's argued that power sharing is a necessary measure in societies divided by segmental cleavages, the dominant ones being race and ethnicity. The two issues, however, should not be seen as providing justification for power sharing because they are not natural or scientific. They are both social constructions and they could be deconstructed for political objectives. History bears testimony to this effect.
Another argument for power sharing is that minorities will be protected against the tyranny of the majority.... It has a lot to do with the small class of wealthy individuals who do not want to lose all the wealth gained from the passed (sic) govt. but to retain it even after they've been defeated in democratic elections.

Destabilization

Power sharing is seen by one respondent as an obstacle to progress because of the ongoing necessity to satisfy all parties:

> Power sharing can never work as a long time solution because there is
> never any long lasting consensus among the different parties involved....
> State resources, which are very tight, need to be utilized more productively
> instead of being wasted on debates which are shaped more by political
> sentiment rather than practical reason and necessity.

Again, the same viewpoint was expressed, but with dire predictions:

> It is a good concept in theory, but in practice leads to more petty disputes
> than actual progress. It would be better to leave the government power
> base to the majority party and when necessary give either a veto power to
> minority parties affected, or allow those affected a chance to decide their
> own issues....I believe there is going to be an explosion onto the political
> scene with the ANC doing away with all possible aspects of power
> sharing, and getting a feel of full-blown power and probably disaster for
> South Africa.

The same note is struck by another respondent who points out that:

> [Power sharing] is an advantage to minority groups in that they are not
> entirely dominated by the policies of the majority parties. It is, however,
> disadvantageous in that the govt. is not particularly stable in proposing
> policies, as with the number of 'power sharers'. There is always bound to
> be some objection to certain aspects of a proposed policy, so resulting in a
> timeous procedure and a weakening in the implementation of policies.

165

In the final analysis, according to one respondent, the overall impact of power sharing is on the economically disadvantaged groups which will continue to suffer because of lack of tangible progress: "Non-progressive parties, e.g. N.P., would use their power to hamper progress - in a sense. Such parties have a tendency to oppose for the sake of opposing development directed to historically disadvantagedcommunities."

Hegemony

The disadvantage of power sharing is that "many white people are reluctant to share; they feel intimidated." The same point is made by another respondent who highlighted the question of white fear and expressed the concern that "the shift is tending towards an imbalance in favor of 'Blacks.' The issue has escalated to one of a political power struggle for dominance where people are seeing things in 'Black and White'."

Power, Privilege and Poverty

The model of power sharing in the South African situation "allows a small economically powerful elite more power than they should have simply because they are in control of the nation's purse strings. This creates a somewhat unequal playing field."

The question of economic power being in the hands of whites seemed to exercise the minds of respondents considerably. Some elaborated at length on this concept:

> The pitfalls around power sharing relate to the extent to which the anticipated fruits of 'uhuru' are not shared equally. It seems that people from a historically disadvantaged background (blacks) still remained dispossessed in a land that is rightly theirs. Meanwhile, those that have

166

been privileged (whites) for centuries are still enjoying the benefits of this 'new' dispensation, more so they have been provided with a mask of a rainbow government behind which they can hide. True reconciliation cannot be realized as long as the social inequities are located along racial lines. Power also relates to material benefits. Where are the advantages?

One respondent points out that the major source of the problem is the South African constitution which has a special clause relating to the protection of minority property rights:

The present political system....serves the interests of (the) white community. The so called black incumbents in the GNU cannot and will not address the problems of (the) majority, black people, who were affected by Apartheid. This is so because of the present constitution adopted by the liberation movements (black) in conjunction with white liberals (NP & DP). For instance, a certain clause in the constitution which reads as "The protection of minority rights." This involves the protection of property rights. One could ask: Who has property? Obviously, white people have property which they have inherited from Apartheid laws. Land is one of the most important property [sic] which any nation will not survive without. Therefore, the RDP with its rhetoric of better housing for all is just a dream. Like Luther who had a dream which later became a nightmare. I am saying this due to unsatisfaction which I experience almost daily in particular, in black communities. Whenever blacks try to put forward or register their demands, our so called leaders in Govt. are the first to criticize those people who are taking action through public demonstrations. They argue thus 'Do not expect things to happen overnight,' or, 'You are making unreasonable demands/expectations.'

While some respondents criticize power sharing arrangements for giving too much power to privileged minority groups, others attack the power elite structure as a whole or those who are seen to be riding the so called gravy train, regardless of race and ethnicity:

> Power sharing - in terms of power - is concentrated in the hands of an elite (black & white) while the average person's life is seldom empowered or improved. The colour of the South African government might have changed but its face is still pretty much the same - rewards are really not reaching the people.

Advantages of Power Sharing

Reconciliation and Peace

Many respondents at the University of Pretoria generally agree that power sharing will bring about a stable society in South Africa. In the view of one respondent power sharing can have the desirable impact because "a more general or even distribution of power will have a peaceful and stable effect on the country."

The impact of power sharing is seen by one respondent to be in the realm of the mind or how people feel about it:

> One of the greatest advantages of power sharing is the psychological effect it has on the collective psyche of the citizens of this country.
> Everybody can feel represented and "to be counting." An important prerequisite for this, however, is that people should trust and have reason to trust the people in Parliament who represent their views (ethnic groups).

Representation and Non Domination

In the new political dispensation of power sharing, "everybody has a say and there are no dominant groups who can force their culture, morals and opinions on the rest of the people."

In the view of one respondent power sharing is more democratic than majority rule: "Power sharing on a pro-rata basis in terms of elections is a more democratic process than outright majority rule. It will also provide minority groups with a political sense of security knowing that they are being represented."

In the words of another respondent: "Everybody feels represented and, therefore, feels they are part of a whole." And the decision making process is more inclusive: "One political party will not be able to make important decisions without input from other parties. All South Africans are represented this way."

Other African countries where the introduction of democracy was problematic are cited to emphasize the importance of power sharing for South Africa. In this regard one respondent stated:

> [Power sharing] "is essential if we want to avoid a 'one-party democracy'
> - there are too many different cultures that a majority rule would not work
> - S.A. must use other African countries as examples of how things do not
> work because of majority rule - which is not to say that power sharing is
> the answer to everlasting peace.

Power sharing is seen by some respondents as the right prescription for South Africa because there is so much cultural diversity and a plethora of views and beliefs in that country:

I think it is quite important since there are so many various political views, personal beliefs and perspectives. These should all be accommodated and none should be ignored. By ignoring certain cultures, beliefs or views, one is creating a problematic climate. Power sharing is necessary to align all these views together and to allow people to feel that they are being listened to and that they are being represented.

Along the same lines one respondent stated:

In a climate where the rights of all people - including minorities - are emphasized, power sharing provides the opportunity for all voices to be heard, rather than those of the minorities being shouted down by a majority. The majority rule's principle implies that the majority is always right - an assumption disproved time and time again in history.

In the final analysis power sharing is seen by some to be simply a temporary measure to realize the important objective of stability: "Power sharing is good in the meantime! Once stability has however been achieved, shouldn't the best person for the job be in control?"

Experience and Development

There was a strong feeling on the part of some respondents that, in the new South Africa, the historically deprived masses, specifically blacks, receive unwarranted attention at the expense of whites who are presented as better educated and more experienced:

I feel that "the masses" are making unfair demands on the government and private sector. Most of the strikers are demanding a salary higher than

mine - I have two degrees, busy with a third. This does not give me the
right to earn a lot of money, but there must be a balance somewhere.

One respondent saw power sharing as promoting reverse discrimination against
whites:

> Power sharing is now definitely leading to a new type of racism. This time
> black against white - Suddenly there is [sic] so many black people with so
> many degrees. Where do they all come from. People with no knowledge is
> [sic] now being appointed in positions that other people wanted for nearly
> 20 years. And then these people who worked for it for 20 years must be
> the "back up system" for this person with no knowledge.

And emphasizing similar views another states that: "Power sharing can only work
if you have capable people on board and not people placed there because of
favoritism or gravy train experts that are corrupt. Corruption must first be
eliminated. Reversed apartheid is now taking place."

One respondent sees the wide cultural gap between blacks and whites as a major
problem which will impact negatively on white standards:

> I believe different cultures can't work in trust with each other - therefore
> the GNU is not trustworthy. The nonwhite races don't have the high
> standard of principles we have, and, therefore, there will always be
> clashes. Further the high standards will be diminished as time goes by.

Another respondent sees power sharing simply as a convenient tool in the hands
of inexperienced leaders: "Power sharing is very much advantageous to the
present government. Reason being that most of our PM's are inexperienced, their
studies were done practically in silent cells and others hardly have relevant
qualifications for the posts they have "

172

Disadvantages of Power Sharing

Destabilization

Some respondents argued that there can be no easy agreements under the power sharing dispensation because of differences in viewpoints: "The only disadvantage I see is that in our country, we all have different outlooks and most of them radical so that it would be very difficult to get an agreement...."

The inevitable result, in the view of another respondent, is that "time is wasted by petty debates about unimportant details.... It may be difficult to represent everyone's viewpoint and find the best solution that suits everyone."

The same point is emphasized by another respondent who indicated that "most probably the greatest disadvantage of power sharing is that the whole governing process becomes extremely time-consuming. This has a negative influence on the collective psyche, because people don't see anything getting better or really changing."

Hegemony

Many of the respondents focused on what they perceived to be the lack of true leadership qualities due to cultural differences or standards of civilization:

In South Africa we have a small group of 1st world people and a large group of 3rd world people. The problem is that in power sharing, the majority of 3rd world citizens makes decisions with which the 1st world element cannot identify. The social, educational, moral and economic standards in this country is [sic] dropping at an alarming rate since power sharingbegan!

Power sharing is seen by some in terms of one racial group losing and another gaining power: "Power sharing is not understood by all the people. Some think that power sharing means that the black people get all the power and the white people lose all their power."

Hence one respondent mentioned that "because of power sharing, the blacks can do whatever they want to; the white people can't do anything about it."

A sense of pessimism about the future of whites in South Africa is underlined by one respondent: "The blacks are the majority and from my point of view, as a young white female, there is not really a future for whites in South Africa."

The solution, in the view of another, lies in the self-determination of minorities:

> Power sharing is the only way in which we can end up with peace. But self-determination of the various peoples of South Africa will be necessary so as to ensure the protection of minority groups, cultural and spiritual traditions of the various groups, and peaceful neighborly relations. Without the ability to protect that which is dear to every group, power sharing will not succeed for minority groups have too few seats in Parliament to make any difference to the majority party.

UNIVERSITY OF STELLENBOSCH

Advantages of Power Sharing

Reconciliation and Peace

There were relatively fewer comments at the University of Stellenbosch relating to questions of reconciliation and peace. One respondent, however, stated that:

> Due to the diverse nature of South African society and the interdependence between the (many) various groups, power sharing is a necessity for peace and harmony. In my belief, there isn't a political party with a ready made answer/strategy for the various problems in S.A. - especially economical, political problems.... a shared power base is more likely to lead to the greatest happiness of the greatest number of people.

Representation and Non Domination

Power sharing may be seen as too burdensome a system but in the final analysis it does deal with the question of representation:

I don't believe there could be "simple" majority rule here with the current range of political parties.... Power sharing is at least an attempt to get all views represented in Parliament. And it's one way to prevent one party from bulldozing over others again. On the other hand, it's a laborious, bulky system and the ANC is battling with it.... It's understandable why the ANC wants majority rule.

With power sharing, opposition party politics is also effectively neutralized:

"When all major parties are in government, it eliminates the notion of opposition for opposition sake.... Instead of trying to bring the ruling party down the opposition parties are engaged in rebuilding the country and offering constructive criticism."

In the case of divided societies, power sharing is regarded by one respondent to be actually better than simple majority rule:

A consociational democracy is the type of democracy that is best suited for divided societies. Better than majority rule - and the only workable type of democracy in very deeply divided societies. The advantages of the consociational (power sharing) system lie hidden in its very principles:
-government by 'grand coalition' i.e. of all significant groups.
-group autonomy by means of decentralization and federalism based on territory; and
-proportionality with regard to political representation.

The superiority of the power sharing system is also extolled:

Power sharing is a system of government that is far superior to the traditional Party and Opposition government; government based on

176

consensus is more efficient and allows for solutions that could not be accepted on a Party and Opposition system.... Once there is consensus, programs are implemented easily.

UNIVERSITY OF FORT HARE

Advantages of Power Sharing

Reconciliation and Peace

A number of respondents at the University of Fort Hare supported power sharing as a necessary interim measure for peace and reconciliation. However, the respondents also emphasized that, after the transitional period, majority rule should be the norm in the new South Africa:

> To attain peace, stability, development, reconstruction, reconciliation and progress, power sharing is suitable for this period, hence we have the GNU concept. For the next election period the majority must take government into its own hands.

In the view of one respondent, the advantage of power sharing relates to the fact that "we are able to tolerate each other and try to reach a negotiated settlement or consensus when there is difference of opinion." Power sharing is the foundation of reconciliation because "it limits the grudges of the past."

179

Representation and Non Domination

Power sharing will allow "every party and everybody to participate in the governing of the country and not only one party determining what should be done." Democracy will also flourish under the new dispensation because "power sharing is going to further the emphasis on democracy giving each party a democratic representative in the new South Africa." Apart from all parties and their ideas being represented, power sharing also "prevents the abuse of power by the majority party in parliament."

Transition and Continuity

Power sharing is necessary for the South African rainbow nation but must be seen to be only suitable for the transitional period. After the transitional period, however, the emphasis should be on majority rule:

> Power sharing is preferable in certain periods and under some conditions.
> The Africans in this country have been, since the arrival of settlers in
> 1652, under immense and brutal oppression and naked exploitation. It then
> is important that for this transitional period (they) take power sharing,
> however as history unfolds the inevitable will and should happen, that is,
> the majority will rule!

Disadvantages of Power Sharing

Neocolonialism

Power sharing may be necessary for reconciliation and peace but, in the view of one respondent, it has a disadvantage in that "your opponents think that because you are prepared to negotiate issues with them, they think that you are weak minded. But to warn them,.....they should not think that preparedness to engage in

180

negotiations determines the weakness of the mind.... The fact that we are preaching or calling for peace does not mean that we are pacifists."

Destabilization

Power sharing may hold the conflicting parties together but the disadvantage is that "the leaders in the G.N.U. don't have respect for each other; they meant to pursue their own personal interests at the expense of another. The leaders of the minority parties within the cabinet use that platform to convey their party politics."

Power sharing allows the minority parties to undermine or sabotage the plans of the ruling party:

> The disadvantage is that other parties are not in the best interest of reconstructing the country, therefore they have an opportunity of opposing major changes that are proposed by the majority party in Parliament. Other Parliament members would deliberately ignore their duties so that the majority government would be blamed at the end of the day.

One respondent sees power sharing as an illusion and ploy on the part of the majority party to stay on top:

> Power sharing is a concept used by political parties to get a place in Parliament and also to let people believe that all political parties that are in Parliament will share power whereas it is not like that. The leading party takes power to itself and baffles people by saying that power is shared.

But another respondent sees, not the majority party, but the white power structure as the main beneficiary of the power sharing arrangements:

In this country its only the whites who benefited in this power sharing. When the Nationalist Party was in power they were ruling alone. The president of S.A. (Mandela) is just a puppet in the Government of National Unity because the N.P. is still having some power in the sense that there must be a consensus before everything and law must be passed. If they are against something it will not be passed. This country belongs to us (Blacks) and there is no need to share it. The issue of sharing power must not come from them as they were the people who raped us of our country and they oppressed and exploited us. The Black people were supposed to be given a chance of ruling their country on their own.

UNIVERSITY OF CAPE TOWN

Advantages of Power Sharing

Reconciliation and Peace

Power sharing is seen as an important concept for a peaceful and stable South
Africa:

> Power sharing as a first step after democratic elections is good/ideal as it
> introduces the rule of the former oppressed gradually, giving time to the
> former rulers and enabling them to get used to seeing blacks in the areas of
> government and other great positions. This also ensures that the fears of
> the losers are addressed and protected during constitution drafting. It also
> serves as a vehicle for maintaining peace and reconciliation.

Power sharing is seen to be accommodating all citizens of the rainbow nation:

> It serves to ensure that all racial and ethnic groups' interests are well
> represented. Minorities can have a say when it comes to the running of the
> Republic. Most especially in this transitional period, power sharing has

brought about stability. This was paving of a way/path for realization of true democracy and equality amongst the people of South Africa.

The necessity of power sharing for stability during the transitional period is an idea that exercised the minds of the respondents a great deal: "Power sharing is necessary for political stability in the interim period. It was necessary to allay the fears of those who thought a black government will engage in reverse discrimination."

The political stability during the transitional period would be realized, not just by allaying fears on the part of whites in general, but by making it extremely difficult for the right wing to stir up racial conflict:

> As Joe Slovo of the South African Communist Party put [it], power sharing was a necessary step in the South African revolution to neutralize the antagonistic and conservative S. African society elements. They had to be denied their base and support and divided and isolated by splitting them by winning the reasonable elements among them.

The advantages of power sharing are thus summarized by one respondent who stated that power sharing:

- Keeps different political parties together so that they can concentrate on the interests of the country (not on petty party politics).

- It encourages the convergence of thoughts rather than divergence.

- Plays a role in reducing tension among party followers. i.e. If leaders of different political parties are seen to be working together then their followers stimulate that action, and

184

- May play an important role in attracting foreign investment.

Representation and Non Domination

Power sharing enables "all stakeholders to voice their views no matter how small they are. It reduces autocratic leadership. The fact that it's limited to 5 years is only for experimental purposes; but I think so far it is working out so why spoil something that works for something unknown."

Power sharing also helps to stem the exodus of apprehensive whites from South Africa:

> The advantage of power sharing in the current S. Africa is that it gives
> those who perceive themselves as minorities the courage to stay in South
> Africa and contribute positively by their skills (administrative and
> otherwise). It also serves to reduce the political violence that results from
> the incitement by desperate leaders of "minorities".

In the new South Africa, political power must be shared because "in a country like South Africa, having only been non-democratic, it would be difficult really to govern the country by one powerful body."

A similar point is advanced by another respondent:

> The only advantage I can think of is that absolute power can never be
> entrusted to just one man. Power has an element of danger and therefore it
> is best that it is distributed. Human nature being what it is, it is best that
> the power to rule is shared - it is best in the interest of the nation.

Disadvantages of Power Sharing

Neocolonialism

Power sharing may be necessary for tactical purposes only to allay fears, but not to advance democracy as such:

> Power sharing is good only as a tactical and not a principled move. It is
> applied for a particular purpose in the period of transition. For me I have a
> problem with the liberal view of power sharing especially in South Africa
> as it contravenes the very essence of democracy. If we apply power
> sharing to curb white fears only, then that is a problem. It is time that all
> our people, irrespective of race, should stand and transform themselves
> and really supersede their racial barriers which are socially constructed by
> the capitalist system of colonialism.

Political power sharing cannot be separated from economic power sharing. Political power sharing is actually viewed as a major obstacle to economic liberation because "one must always take into account that power sharing is 180 degrees different from economic power sharing. I believe that most of the deprived masses would never be liberated if the economy lies in the hands of less than one percent of the total population."

One respondent even went further and stated that the masses will in fact be kept in their state of perpetual poverty as a result of the power sharing pact between former forces of the liberation movement and former oppressors:

> It is just a system to keep the African, especially the working class
> and peasants, in perpetual bondage. Any efforts by the so called former
> liberation movements will be thwarted by the traditional white parties and

the mainly white civil service. It is a forced marriage between the "masters" and their slaves, engineered by foreign powers only interested in exploiting the country's resources e.g. mines. It appears good because it stops the greedy politician from challenging the government, because everyone is having a slice of the cake. African leaders are made to preside over a preplanned program whose aim is to freely exploit the working class without [a] guilty conscience.

From the point of view of another respondent, power sharing should not have been allowed at all because nothing good can be expected from former oppressors:

I am totally against the GNU. I still do not think that [the] ANC should have allowed this to happen. The NP and the rest of the apartheid regime made a mess of South Africa (and they are still continuing); and now they think they can aid the ANC in "cleaning up" the mess. What they are (NP + DP + IFP) actually doing is passing as an obstacle/barrier to the progress of this country. The power sharing is a concept that will never work, simply because not all the parties in the GNU want to make South Africa a better, democratic "debtless" country fit to compete in the international world. Viva majority rule Viva!

Destabilization

Power sharing is guaranteed to cause unnecessary problems for the ruling party. Majority rule seems to be the answer:

First, let me correct the term. It should be power struggle. How can dozens of political organizations govern. Let me give you a scenario: Suppose the ANC proposes a reconstruction of all African townships with minimal payment by residents. What do you anticipate the NP would say? Surely,

187

they will talk about cutting government expenditure involving the private sector and so forth. Who gains at the end? The very same "old big bosses." Just now the RDP has not even surfaced because they keep arguing about technicalities. On the other hand, IFP want autonomy so they threaten to pull out of Parliament.. Right now the constitution is likely to be challenged by the IFP because it is being drafted at their absence. So it becomes a circular spiral of complexities. One organization governing by majority rule would have made a lot of progress. Now no one can take the blame for anything, because everyone is there, at least they are supposed to be there! pss [sic]. They do not attend Parliamentary sessions - they are paid for wining and dining around the country!

The undue leverage that minority parties are supposed to have is viewed as a major destabilizing factor. And when that power is taken away, a resurgence of conflict is likely to occur. Therefore, the disadvantages of power sharing are:

- the views of the majorities are held back by those who profess to be expressing views of the "minorities" which should be protected.
- the government can justify its inability to deliver by saying the leaders of "minorities" are holding them back.
- when the elections come again a decision has to be taken whether to stick to or abandon power sharing.
- In the event it is abandoned then the violence that was temporarily suspended by leaders of "minorities" will be sparked again.

It is also a question of conservative elements making it difficult for progressive programs intended to help the disadvantaged to be implemented:

Power sharing meant that the situation in the country won't change, because the conservatives have the power to block/ veto programs designed to improve the conditions of previously excluded groups i.e. blacks and females. It also means that those who don't abide by the interim constitution are not fired because they are guaranteed their jobs through the power sharing agreement.

There is also the problem of sharing power with former leaders who do not want reform and never showed any remorse for the evils of the apartheid regime:

There is widespread paralysis and lack of progress in issues such as Land Reform (redistribution), redistribution of wealth and apartheid criminals like PW Botha, de Klerk and other NP leaders go around arrogantly despite having led the raping of all the black society.

PART III

CONCLUSION

14

CONCLUSION

This study focused on the attitudes of final year university students to the concepts of power sharing, equality, democracy and other related issues in the new South Africa. The study was based on an analysis of responses from 930 final year university students. This represents a little over 2% sample of the 27,783 student body at the nine South African universities targeted. Three traditionally black universities, four traditionally white (two English speaking and two Afrikaans speaking) universities, one traditionally Colored university and one traditionally Indian university were included in the study.

The quantitative section of the study dealt with a set of structured questions designed to elucidate the many sides of power sharing, the political process and dissent in the new, post apartheid, South Africa. Although there are many points of cleavage in the polity of South Africa, the survey results received many points of consensus among the university students. Indeed, on some crucial issues, black and white (English speaking and Afrikaners), Colored and Indian respondents adopted very similar points of view. The respective positions of individual universities were also highlighted, whenever pertinent or necessary, for comparative purposes and, especially, to pinpoint a significant deviation from the national pattern of responses. In the section focusing on the only open-ended question relating to power sharing, excerpts from each individual university were analyzed to underline the position of each university on the question of power sharing and related matters. The open-ended question gave the respondents an opportunity to state their views ad libitum and provided insights that could not be obtained through structured questions.

The concept of power sharing, involving the black and white sections of the South African population, is new in the turbulent history of the country. After the historic 1994 national elections power sharing was advocated by the ruling elites as a necessary foundation for reconciliation, peace and stability. The views of university students, from whose ranks will most likely emerge the future political elites and leaders of the new South Africa, were spelled out clearly on the question of power sharing.

The majority of respondents (51%) were strongly in favor of power sharing in the new South Africa and a significant number (36%) were moderately in favor of it. Power sharing was so strongly favored by the respondents that it was considered by an even greater majority (70%) to be a better basis for democracy than majority rule.

There are good reasons why power sharing received such strong support from the respondents. The country had just emerged from a long period of racial oppression, political violence and social instability as a result of the apartheid system and there was an imperative need, following the first nonracial elections in the history of the country, to move in an alternative direction of reconciliation, peace and stability. The majority of responses supported the view that power sharing was necessary for reconciliation (73%), for peace (77%), and for stability (67%). These high figures clearly show why the respondents found power sharing at this critical juncture in the history of South Africa to be a better basis for democracy than majority rule. If reconciliation, peace and stability are indeed of paramount importance, then power sharing at this transitional phase is a better basis for democracy than majority rule.

From a qualitative perspective, the preponderance of individual responses to the open ended question on power sharing also confirms the majority viewpoint indicated by the high quantitative numbers. In response to the open ended question on power sharing, the majority of comments from respondents in each university were positive and in favor of the new political dispensation of power sharing.

On the positive side, many respondents emphasized the advantages of power sharing for peace and reconciliation in a multiracial and heterogeneous country like South Africa. The point was made a number of times that, through power sharing, blacks and whites would be kept together, particularly during the critical transitional period when the different groups were adjusting to change. Power sharing was seen as the most accommodating system because it allowed different ethnic and racial groups to be equally and democratically represented in the new power structure. It was needed for peace, reconciliation, harmony and stability which were necessary conditions for reconstruction and development.

In view of the history of racial and ethnic domination that was typical of the apartheid era, many respondents welcomed the idea of representation that was inherent in the power sharing arrangement. Political representation of all groups was necessary to avoid the domination of one group by another that was the hallmark of the apartheid system. In the new South Africa, the black majority was now in charge and whites were now the numerical minority. Power sharing was, therefore, necessary to allay the fears of whites who thought a black government would resort to reverse discrimination against whites. In the final analysis, power sharing had the overall effect of softening the blow of the black majority government and democracy on those who never wanted or were not prepared for fundamental change. In other words, power sharing had a positive effect on the collective psyche of the nation because the different ethnic and racial groups felt represented and not dominated.

The point was also emphasized by some respondents that blacks needed whites for their experience, if the country was to move forward with effective and efficient development. The apartheid system had deliberately denied blacks the opportunity to receive proper education and technical skills that would enable them to compete effectively with whites in the labor market. Power sharing arrangements made certain that whites would continue to contribute their share to the development of the country.

The apartheid system saw to it that blacks were also not allowed to participate in national politics, a domain reserved exclusively for whites. This meant that blacks were denied the opportunity to be experienced in the technicalities of national government. This point was recognized by respondents who argued that power sharing was necessary to maintain a smooth transition and continuity in governance. Whites were experienced in the affairs of national politics and power sharing allowed them to contribute their knowledge and skills in the running of the new South Africa.

On the negative side, power sharing was viewed by respondents as meaningful only in political and not economic terms. Many viewed the new power sharing arrangement as a perpetuation of neocolonialism. The point was made by a number of respondents that, for the black majority, political power sharing did not translate into economic power sharing because economic power in the new South Africa was still effectively centered in white hands. The historically disadvantaged masses may be politically liberated, but they are still economically deprived and powerless. From this perspective, power sharing is viewed as a system that is addressing white fears rather than dealing with the problem of uplifting those who were kept down by white minority rule. The new black majority government may be determined to improve the lot of the poor but, because of political power sharing, it is destabilized and handicapped in its efforts to implement policies relating to reconstruction and development. The black rulers may be in office but not in power and therefore can not deliver and fulfill promises made to the black majority. The impact of power sharing is, therefore, to hold democracy at ransom and to derail the will of the majority.

The respondents also felt that the question of poverty would not be effectively addressed by the political elites because the ruling class, now made up of whites and blacks, is actually more interested in maintaining its position of power and privilege than in dealing with structural inequities. And, because of hegemonic tendencies on the part of participants in the power sharing structure, it is difficult to reach the consensus that is required to make meaningful structural changes.

The views on the open ended question relating to power sharing were expressed without any restrictions by the respondents and, therefore, added an important qualitative dimension to the quantitative responses on structured questions. The numbers and percentages relating to structured questions indicate how many respondents were for or against power sharing but the opinions freely expressed certainly cast an important light, not only on the depth of feelings and emotions surrounding the issue, but also on the rationale and implications of sharing power in the new South Africa.

In their quantitative responses, the respondents not only thought highly about the crucial role of power sharing during the transitional period but a significant number of them (50%) also felt that power sharing should be extended beyond the limited period of five years. And, by an even larger majority (57%), the respondents endorsed the idea that power sharing should be a permanent feature of the South African political structure.

The general pattern of responses, therefore, seems to indicate, not only strong support for the idea of power sharing, but also for its extension and even incorporation as a permanent element of the South African political system. The level of that support, however, is either high or low depending on the particular university.

A comparative analysis of the respective positions of the individual universities on power sharing gives us a better picture of the depth of the support for the concept in the different institutions.

In the traditionally black universities, support for power sharing is higher than 50% but in traditionally white, Indian and Colored universities, that support falls below 50%. The less support for power sharing on the part of traditionally white, Indian and Colored universities, as compared to traditionally black universities, could be an indication that there might still be some residual fear on the part of the minority groups (white, Colored and Indian) in the face of the power of the black majority. After all, the ANC, which received overwhelming support from the majority of blacks, was the senior and dominant partner in the government of National Unity. In other words, even though power sharing may be a welcome arrangement for minority groups because it is inclusive and gives them a voice in the political process, it may also imply domination of minorities by those who wield more political power.

The principle of majority rule, when juxtaposed with the policy of power sharing, sheds more light on the possible reason why power sharing received less support, on a comparative basis, from minority group universities than from majority group universities.

198

The idea that power sharing was a better basis for democracy than majority rule received enthusiastic support from minority respondents. The preference for this political arrangement on the part of these minority respondents was over 50% and ranged from 55% to 90%. The principle of majority rule explicitly denotes the concept of power in larger numbers and, when introduced, power sharing becomes more of an attractive option for the traditionally white, Colored and Indian universities than absolute majority rule. Therefore, it appears to be the overwhelming numbers of blacks that may be the source of concern for minority groups that may now have a say in power sharing but may likely be left out in the cold in the strict application of the principle of majority rule. Hence the fear of majority rule which, in the view of minority groups, may imply black majority rule and possibly black domination. But power sharing is seen to be a better basis for democracy by both majority and minority groups because, at least during the transitional period, it contributes to reconciliation, peace and stability. From this perspective, it is seen by the respondents to be a good thing for the new South Africa.

The principle of majority rule, which is universally recognized as an integral part of the democratic process, was supported only by 44% of the respondents in the sample. This comes as no surprise because the results are consistent with the view endorsed by the respondents that power sharing is a better basis for democracy than majority rule. There is a difference, however , in the relative positions taken by individual universities on the question of majority rule.

The majority opinion (i.e. over 50%) in all three black universities was in support of the principle of majority rule and so was the case at the University of the Western Cape and the University of Cape Town. The support for the principle at the University of Durban-Westville was less than 50%. The University of the Witwatersrand, the University of Pretoria and the University of Stellenbosch expressed more reservation than support for the idea of majority rule. Therefore,

199

the concept of majority rule, with the exception of all three black universities, did not receive overall majority support as compared to power sharing.

There was also no general agreement on the inevitability of absolute black majority rule. A sizeable number of respondents (43%) expressed uncertainty about the whole idea, although there was a significant agreement by a number of respondents (43%) that black majority rule will amount to black domination. Opinions on this question of possible black domination was mostly divided, at individual universities, between those who did not accept or were uncertain about the idea and some who agreed that black rule will amount to black domination. There was no majority opinion expressed on this question, except at the University of Durban-Westville (52%), the University of Pretoria (72%) and the University of Stellenbosch (60%), which all agreed that black rule will amount to black domination in the new South Africa. This firm position taken by minority group universities that black majority rule will amount to black domination provides a logical explanation why the majority of respondents have a strong preference for power sharing as a better basis for democracy than absolute majority rule. The possibility of black domination, which is implicit in absolute majority rule, is a source for concern and apprehension, particularly on the part of minority groups.

The question of political power and the form it could take in the new South Africa was addressed in terms of the three political systems proposed for the new South Africa , namely, a unitary structure in which political power is centralized, a federal structure in which power is decentralized through devolution to the nine provinces and a consociational structure in which power is shared by racial and ethnic groups that have communal autonomy and veto rights to protect their interests.

200

A sizeable number of respondents (43%) showed a higher preference for a unitary system followed, in the second place, by a smaller number of those (36%) who preferred a federal system. This pattern of preference was repeated in the individual universities. The only exceptions were the University of Pretoria and the University of Stellenbosch which registered a higher preference for a federal political system. Again, the choice of Afrikaner respondents at the two universities could have been influenced by the possibility of black domination because, for them, a unitary political structure meant loss of power in a system that would be under the control of the black majority. In a federal structure, there was room for minority groups because of decentralization, devolution and retention of some political power.

A unitary structure, followed by a federal structure, was also the collective choice (37%), albeit weak, of the respondents. It was viewed as a political system that is ideal for better race relations. An even weaker preference (31%) was shown for a unitary structure, followed in the second position by a federal structure, as a system that is ideal for different ethnic groups.

A unitary structure was also the first collective choice of respondents (41%) in terms of being an ideal political system for democracy in South Africa. The exceptions were both Afrikaans speaking universities that opted for the federal system as their first choice of a political system that is ideal for democracy. As minority group universities, the preference for a federal structure as an ideal system for democracy is consistent with the desire to retain some form of political power within the system.

The respondents not only showed greater preference for a unitary political system as ideal for race, ethnicity and democracy but a sizeable number of them (36%) thought a unitary system should be entrenched in the new South African constitution. The only exceptions were both Afrikaans speaking universities which gave first and greater support to a federal system.

The choice by the majority of respondents of a unitary structure as ideal for better racial and ethnic relations as well as for democracy, and the advocacy for a constitutional entrenchment of such a system, does make a great deal of sense in a country that was plagued by racial and ethnic divisions under the apartheid system of government. A unitary system is by definition the antithesis of the apartheid system which was characterized by racial domination and ethnic fragmentation. But in terms of the concept of power sharing, a federal political system makes a great deal of sense also, particularly for minority groups, because, by definition, it means devolution and decentralization of political power and thus it makes it a logical first choice of the Afrikaans speaking universities.

Since political parties and their leaders have a major role to play in the political process, whatever type of political system characteristic of the new South Africa will depend ultimately on the definitive role of the ruling party or parties elevated to power by the electorate.

The collective choice of the respondents in the April 1994 all-race elections was overwhelmingly for the ANC (58%). In terms of individual universities, the ANC was the party of first choice at both English speaking universities, all three black universities, the Indian university and the Colored university. The Nationalist Party was the undisputed winner at the University of Pretoria and the University of Stellenbosch.

On the face of it, the results relating to the choice of political parties might suggest that race and ethnicity played a role in the preferences of the respondents, especially in view of the fact that the two major antagonistic groups in the history

202

of South Africa, blacks and Afrikaners, voted solidly for the ANC and the NP respectively. But this assumption was rejected by the respondents who made it clear that neither race or ethnicity had anything to do with their political preferences. What the majority of respondents (62%) agreed about was that the first nonracial election in the history of South Africa was, in the final analysis, about getting rid of the apartheid system and that the test for true democracy would be in subsequent elections, an idea that was supported by a majority (51%) of the respondents. This view may explain the fact that a year later after the 1994 elections, when this survey was conducted, the overall support for the ANC, whilst retaining its position as the most favored political party, had fallen about ten points from 58% to 48%. This pattern of decreased preference for the ANC was repeated in almost all universities. The only notable exceptions were the University of Pretoria where the ANC gained 2% and the University of Stellenbosch where it gained 5%. That shifting pattern of voting preferences underscored the viewpoint that the issue now and for the future is no more apartheid but how the leaders of the new democratic South Africa can deliver on election promises. The respondents may therefore have a point in their collective view that the true test of democracy in the new South Africa lies in future elections.

As far as the national elections were concerned, the respondents made it clear that matters of race and ethnicity played no role in their political preferences. The majority of respondents also indicated that their first choice of a political system was a unitary structure which was considered ideal for better racial and ethnic relations. These views are actually in line with their opinions on the question of racial equality under the law. The majority of respondents (70%) were "definitely in favor" of racial equality under the law - a cardinal principle of the new South African constitution. However, a significant number of the respondents (43%) stated that blacks were still not receiving equal treatment under the law. Also, in terms of future projections, there was less enthusiastic support for the idea that racial equality would be realized in South Africa, although a sizeable number felt it was possible (43%).

In terms of a possible time frame, respondents projected that it would take "decades" (38%) or "years" (29%) before racial equality could be realized in South Africa. But since the law in South Africa is categorically for nonracialism, those views on racial equality may be more of a reflection of the residual stereotypical attitudes between blacks and whites, which may be reinforced by the large socio-economic gap between the rich and the poor (i.e. whites and blacks), than a realistic portrayal of the current status of blacks under the new South African constitution.

In the same vein, with regard to the question of ethnicity, the respondents were "definitely in favor" (49%) of ethnic equality which all ethnic groups were entitled to have under the new South African laws. But again, to endorse the idea of ethnic equality is not the same as saying that ethnic equality is or will become a reality in the new South Africa. On this question, only 38% of the respondents thought that ethnic equality could "possibly" be realized in their country. Moreover, the time frame for the realization of that ethnic equality is estimated, like in the case of racial equality, to be in "decades" (35%) or "years" (28%).

Therefore, although all racial and ethnic groups are accorded an equal status under the constitution, the views of the respondents on equality point to a clear recognition that, despite the new political and legal order, South Africa is still a racially and ethnically stratified society and may remain like that for a long time to come.

If there was any doubt at all about exactly what exercised the minds of the respondents when they expressed their views on the state of legal equality between blacks and whites in the racial and ethnic spheres, their opinions on the economic gap between these two population groups seem to leave no room for lingering doubts about the state of inequality in the new South Africa. There was a high degree of agreement on the part of respondents (82%) that, because of the legacy of apartheid, the majority of whites in South Africa have a greater economic power than blacks. That perspective was supported by all universities without exception, even though there was a difference of opinion about how exactly to quantify that economic gap between whites and blacks. The majority of respondents (55%) characterized the gap as being "very large." The only exception was the University of Pretoria which, whilst agreeing with the general viewpoint about the existence of the gap, described it as being just "large."

In terms of expectations about the future gap, the results were spread out and not indicative of any clear pattern of responses. But, as far as the present was concerned, there was a majority agreement (55%) that political power sharing did not in fact translate into economic power sharing. In other words, the black majority have less economic power than the white minority.

If there was general agreement on the part of respondents that political power sharing did not necessarily mean economic power sharing, there was no majority opinion, however, on one of the suggested ways of closing the gap between the haves and the havesnot, namely, equitable distribution of wealth through higher taxation aimed at the rich. A better picture only emerges when we look at the combination of those who were "definitely in favor" (21%) and "in favor" (32%) of higher taxes for the rich. In this case, a significant majority (53%) were either definitely in favor or just in favor of that policy. From this angle of tabulation, the majority of the respondents (53%) favored higher taxes for the rich, as compared to those who were against (46%) such higher taxes. The only exceptions to this general pattern of responses were the University of Zululand, which took an ambivalent position on the issue, and the Afrikaans speaking universities, which were firmly against the distribution of wealth through higher taxes for the rich.

There were dissenting views on the question of bridging the gap between the rich and the poor through higher taxes for the rich, but there was agreement by the majority of the respondents (65%) that the state of economic inequality in South Africa had a potential for racial conflict. And, as if confirming the confluence between race and class, an almost equal majority of the respondents (64%) agreed that there is also a potential for class conflict in South Africa, if present economic inequities continue. Therefore both race and class inequalities are viewed with equal gravity and concern by the respondents who see a great potential for conflict in both areas, unless something is done to bridge the socio-economic gulf between the rich and the poor (i.e. whites and blacks) in South Africa.

The response of the GNU to the problem of socio-economic disparities was to promote growth and development through the business sector. The new government argued that the business sector was not to be overburdened with higher taxes, if more jobs were to be created to improve the economic status of blacks. That policy of the GNU was supported by a significant number of the respondents (49%), although a large number of them (44%) also expressed reservations about its effectiveness.

That same feeling of doubt and skepticism was directed towards the RDP in terms of its effectiveness in narrowing the gap between the rich and poor in South Africa. Whilst a good number of the respondents thought it was "possible" (50%) that the RDP would deliver, a significant number (32%) were "doubtful" that the socio-economic gap could be narrowed through the RDP. If the RDP did not succeed to narrow or close the gap between the rich and the poor, a number of respondents (45%) thought it was "possible" that a major conflict would ensue in the country. Also, due to the rampant poverty in the black section of the population, 46% of the respondents thought that the crime rate would rise. The respondents therefore left no doubt that the ramifications of poverty could have serious consequences

The war on poverty in South Africa is waged within the framework of the capitalist system and only 38% of the respondents thought it was "possible" that the Western style market economy could succeed in narrowing the gap between the rich and the poor, and 38% thought it was "doubtful" the capitalist system could deliver. But there was also little support for the idea that the government should use nationalization to realize its objective of equity. A significant number of respondents (46%) were "uncertain" that nationalization would work at all. Under the apartheid regime, nationalization, as advocated by the liberation movement, was always demonized and associated with the extremes of socialism. The views of the respondents may be a reflection of that systemic denigration.

The idea that socialism, the ideological alternative to capitalism, could succeed where capitalism has failed received a mixed reaction from the different universities. But the combined views (54%) of those who said it was "possible" (30%) and those who were in favor of socialism (24%) seem to suggest that socialism has a better chance than capitalism to reduce the gap between the rich and the poor. There was however no clear majority opinion in support of socialism as a better alternative to capitalism.

The most significant result of the survey relating to the possible consequences for the new South Africa, if the government is not successful in uplifting the living conditions of the majority of poor blacks, is that, in the view of the majority of the respondents (52%), the climate of peace and goodwill that was ushered into the country after the April 1994 elections would not continue.

In its eagerness to promote economic growth and development, the Government of National Unity called upon workers, particularly blacks, to tighten their belts in order to help the government to realize its major objective. This policy received majority support (58%) from the respondents but, as far as implementation of the policy was concerned, an even larger majority (68%) of respondents were against denying workers more wages in order to maintain high productivity. Therefore, in theory, the respondents were in support of belt tightening but, in practice, they were opposed to the implementation of the policy to the historically disadvantaged and poorly paid black workers.

A large majority of the respondents (66%) expressed the view that the militant black workers would not wait for economic growth and development before forging ahead with strike action for better wages. This opinion, however, was not an indication that the respondents were for strike action per se because their support for strike action was divided and took the form of "reservations." But there was no question that they were strongly in support of the interests of workers and, from that point of view, a significant number of them (48%) were opposed to the proposition that, in the event of a strike, employers should have the constitutional right to lock out striking workers. The only two exceptions to this general viewpoint were the University of Pretoria, where a larger majority (77%) were in support of the lock out proposition, and the University of Stellenbosch where a significant number (45%) agreed that employers should have the right to lock out workers. The majority of universities made it clear that the interests of workers can not be sacrificed to government policies, however laudable these may appear to be.

The GNU embarked on the policy of affirmative action to enable blacks to have better opportunities for employment but this policy drew mixed reactions form the respondents, albeit more on the positive side. A number of respondents were

208

either "strongly in favor" (38%) or just "in favor" (35%) of affirmative action. This general pattern was repeated in the majority of individual universities. The two English speaking universities, the three black universities and the Colored University of the Western Cape had more respondents who were "strongly in favor" of affirmative action to correct historical injustices. At the University of Stellenbosch more respondents were simply "in favor" of that policy. On the negative side, the University of Durban-Westville and the University of Pretoria had more respondents who were "strongly against" affirmative action.

The respondents were also divided in their views on the question of whether affirmative action serves the unintended purpose of portraying blacks as unqualified workers in the eyes of white workers. The responses were divided almost evenly between those who said affirmative action would not (36%) portray black workers as unqualified workers and those who agreed (33%) that blacks would be viewed as unqualified workers. The respondents were also divided almost evenly in their opinions on whether white workers would be justified in viewing affirmative action as reverse discrimination. A good number (37%) agreed that white workers would be justified to think that there was reverse discrimination and 38% said there would be no justification for such thinking.

The respondents could not agree on the effect of affirmative action on race relations and were evenly divided between those who thought that affirmative action would contribute to bad race relations (36%) and those who said race relations would not be affected (35%) by affirmative action. Affirmative action is undoubtedly a controversial issue and hence the views of the respondents on its effects or implications were divided and at best ambivalent.

The question of less qualifications would probably not arise if blacks, from elementary level schools to universities, had been exposed to the same quality of education as whites. To bring blacks to the same level of quality education as

209

whites would require a radical transformation of the educational system in South Africa. Overall, the majority of respondents "agree" or "strongly agree" (92%) that the educational system in South Africa needs radical transformation to enable blacks to get good education, which is the basis for rapid upward mobility.

The inequality in education began at black schools which were rated by the respondents as either "poor" (40%) or "very poor" (37%). This evaluation of black schools contrasts very sharply with that of white schools which were rated by the respondents to be "excellent" (49%) or "good" (41%). The gap between whites and blacks in the field of education is therefore an issue of paramount importance which is accordingly acknowledged by the respondents.

Black universities were also not regarded with high esteem and were rated by the majority of the respondents to be either "fair" (38%) or "poor" "30%), as compared to the traditionally white universities which were rated as either "excellent" (47%) or "good" (44%).

There can therefore be no question that education in South Africa, from primary level to universities, needs radical transformation if blacks are to be in a better position to compete fairly and effectively within the system.

Power sharing had a dramatic impact on the number of official languages in South Africa where the indigenous African languages were elevated to the level of the two other official languages, Afrikaans and English, resulting in a total of eleven official languages. The respondents seemed satisfied with the status quo and were either "in favor" (33%) or "strongly in favor" (26%) of it. But whether the overall interests of the country are better served by such an unprecedented number of official languages is another matter.

210

A significant number of respondents either "agreed" or "strongly agreed" (54%) with the statement that the national interests of the country would be better served by one official language. In response to the proposal of elevating English as the only official language, 63% of the respondents were either "for" or "definitely for" English as the only official language in South Africa. If it should require a national referendum to decide on whether English should be the only official language, 68% of the respondents were either "for" or "definitely for" the idea of such a referendum. Furthermore, 72% of the respondents indicated they would either "accept" or "definitely accept" the results of such a decision.

The elevation of English as the only official language in South Africa would of course mean that the other languages would lose their official status or be demoted in stature from a higher to a lower level.

A high number of respondents (42%) did not think that the acceptance of English as the only official language would necessarily amount to a demotion of other languages. However, a significant number (31%) agreed with the statement that the recognition of English as the only official language would in effect mean a demotion to the language of each ethnic group in South Africa.

The question of the official language aside, the respondents took a very clear position on the legal right of languages to exist in South Africa. A significant number of respondents (27%) were for " the right of different racial and ethnic groups to preserve and maintain their own languages" and a majority of them (52%) were "very much" in support of that legal right. Therefore, the respondents made it clear that, even if a decision to have one official language could be nationally supported, all ethnic languages must continue to have their legal right to exist.

In the new South Africa there are also two national anthems. The existence of the two national anthems, like the eleven official languages, also received support from the respondents who were either "moderately in favor" (36%) or "strongly in favor" (25%) of the two national anthems.

The respondents were also either "moderately in favor" (34%) or "strongly in favor" (25%) of an amalgamated national anthem which would include parts selected from both anthems.

The preponderance of views was therefore in favor of the two national anthems or an amalgamated version of the same two anthems. The marriage of convenience between the anthem of former oppressors and the anthem of former freedom fighters was certainly a very unusual and extraordinary event. It can only be understood in the broader context of the spirit of peace, stability and reconciliation that the respondents so strongly supported.

Power sharing was possible and became a reality in the new and democratic South Africa. There can be no question that it has taken determined and courageous leadership to pull South Africa out of the iron jaws of the apartheid system. On the white side, F.W. de Klerk, as the president of the country and leader of the Nationalist Party, was faced with the daunting task of presiding over the demise of the notorious apartheid system. The respondents acknowledged his contribution to the dismantling process at a critical juncture in the history of the country. A high number of them (61%) agreed that F.W. de Klerk played a major role in convincing the majority of white South Africans to abandon apartheid and turn their attention to the politics of negotiations. The majority of respondents (63%) also made it clear that de Klerk had played an important role in persuading the white electorate to accept change. The leadership role of de Klerk was therefore strongly acknowledged by the respondents.

If de Klerk was recognized for his leadership in convincing the majority of whites to abandon the sinking apartheid ship, Nelson Mandela received even higher recognition for his historic role in the struggle for a free and just society. As an outstanding leader, he received the highest rating (88%) for his major contribution to the struggle for freedom and justice in South Africa. The majority of the respondents (65%) also agreed with the statement that, after his inauguration as president, Nelson Mandela did much to restore confidence in democracy in South Africa. He was not only highly recognized for his historic role before and after the elections, but a high number of respondents (70%) believed that he was in fact the social glue that kept whites and blacks together in the new South Africa.

It is because of the special and preeminent role played by Nelson Mandela in holding the disparate elements of the South African population together that the respondents registered concern about the future of the country after his presidency. The apprehension ranged from "slight" (35%) to "moderate" 27%) to "very much" (23%).

To summarize, the relative racial harmony in the new South Africa can be attributed primarily to the stabilizing presence of Nelson Mandela. The country will eventually have to find ways of managing without the dominant voice behind power sharing, equality and democracy. It remains to be seen what it will take to realize that major objective.

PART IV

APPENDIXES

(A)

METHODOLOGY

The study focused on the attitudes of final year university students to the concepts of power-sharing, equality and democracy in South Africa in the aftermath of the country's historic transformation from the system of legalized racism called apartheid to a non-racial and democratic society.

A government of national unity, based on the transitional power-sharing constitution, was in office for a year when the study was conducted in 1995. The purpose of the study was to test the power-sharing formula and related questions in one major and significant group, the university student population from whose ranks would most likely emerge the future rulers of the country. The research targeted final year students whose long educational background at university level would have equipped them with the necessary intellectual and analytical tools to comprehend the questionnaire and provide lucid and meaningful responses. But the question could rightly be raised: Why final year students? The answer to that legitimate question lies in the fact that the researcher, who had previous personal experience of the poor quality of education at the university level in the traditionally black universities***, was genuinely concerned that students below the final year level at those universities would most probably experience real difficulties in dealing with the questionnaire and hence submit responses that would not be enlightening or even approximate the level of sophistication typical of the traditionally white universities.

To obtain the views of the students, a questionnaire consisting of one hundred questions was constructed. The questions covered the following major categories:

1. Power Sharing (11 questions)
2. Political Parties (7 questions)
3. Equality (4 questions)
4. Ethnicity (8 questions)
5. Democracy (12 questions)
6. Economy (15 questions)
7. Workers (6 questions)
8. Affirmative Action (4 questions)
9. Education (7 questions)
10. Language (7 questions)
11. National Anthem (2 questions)
12. Leaders (6 questions)
13. Background Information (11 questions)

The target of the study was a random sample of 2% or more of 27783, the total number of the 1995 final year students in the nine selected universities.

The following is the list of universities covered in the study:

Name of the institution	1995 Finalists	Respondents	Percent
The University of the North	1845	238	12.9
University of Zululand	1293	152	11.8
University of Fort Hare	1515	43	2.8
University of the Western Cape	3464	78	2.3
University of Durban-Westville	2553	31	1.2
University of the Witwatersrand	3750	99	2.6
University of Cape Town	5330	59	1.1
University of Pretoria	5483	210	3.8
University of Stellenbosch	2550	20	0.8
TOTAL	27783	930	3.3

As noted, the objective of the survey was to obtain at least 2 percent of responses from each university. The main body of the questionnaire was made up of questions focusing specifically on the central concepts of power sharing, equality, democracy and related matters. The final section of the questionnaire was designed to cover basic demographic information relating to age, gender, marital status,

219

children, education, religion, class, residence and the name of the university of each respondent. The demographic information was, however, not useful in shedding more light on the central questions of the study and was therefore excluded from the evaluation of the research data.

The pretesting of survey questions on a small sample of final year students was done at the University of the North, where I was based for my research. This phase of the work was followed by the actual study, conducted at each of the nine universities. I was personally responsible for the gathering of information at the University of the North but, in the case of the other eight universities, I depended on other research assistants, mainly professors, who volunteered their services to administer the questionnaire to final year students.

To anticipate and minimize the problem of poor returns, an additional 100 questionnaires, over and above the total number of students represented by 2%, were submitted to each participating university. This proved to be a correct adjustment because in none of the targeted universities was there a 100% return of completed questionnaires. In the end, a total of 930 respondents was realized and that number amounted to 3.3% of the total number of final year students in the nine universities.

The responses to all structured questions were clear and to the point. The only exception was question number 23 which dealt with ethnicity and race. In response to that question, many students were simply not willing to state who they were in terms of their membership in an ethnic, cultural or racial group. They would simply state "I am South African." This pattern of responses may have been a reflection of the general mood of the country to move away from ethnic and racial categorizations towards what was constantly projected by the new political leaders as the new nonracial and nonsexist society.

220

Questions 23 through to 27 were not part of the original set of structured questions but were included later at the request of a researcher at the Human Science Research Council in Pretoria who was interested in the role of culture and ethnicity in South Africa. These questions, which required intricate and multifaceted responses, were not helpful in the final analysis and were therefore excluded from the evaluation of data relating to the central concepts of power sharing, equality and democracy.

Question number 11, which dealt with power sharing, was the only open ended question and the responses to it were therefore unstructured. This question was introduced to give students an opportunity to state their views on power sharing without the limitations imposed by structured questions.

Since the study was conducted a year after the first all-race elections in the history of the country, it was not only distinctive in terms of originality and focus, but it also had the added advantage of analyzing attitudes relating to a new and fundamentally different political dispensation. In terms of scope, it was a comprehensive study because it covered not only the whole racial spectrum relating to historically black, white, Indian and Colored universities, but also dealt with nine different universities ranging, in terms of racial representation and inclusiveness, from the non-integrated to the relatively most integrated.

*** The author was a Pharmacy student at the University of the North in 1972 and was one of a number of students who voluntarily withdrew from the university after a general boycott of classes to protest the expulsion of A.O.R. Tiro, a prominent and highly respected SASO leader.

(B)

QUESTIONNAIRE

Attitudes toward Power-sharing, Racial Equality and Democracy in South Africa: A Study of South African University Students

Introduction

The aim of this study is to gather information about the attitudes of final year university students towards power-sharing, racial equality, democracy and other related matters. There are no true or false answers. This is a scientific research conducted by a sociologist from the University of Massachusetts Dartmouth in collaboration with a researcher from the Social Dynamics Group at the Human Sciences Research Council in Pretoria. The information obtained from the investigation will be used for scientific objectives and will serve as an important data source for academicians, scholars, lawmakers, policy makers and political leaders. Please feel free to give responses that reflect your true opinions.

Power Sharing

1. The concept of power-sharing is explained as government by consensus among the participating political groups. To what extent are you in favor or against power-sharing in South Africa?

   1 Strongly in favor   2 Moderately in favor

   3 Moderately against   4 Strongly against

2. In a racially and ethnically divided country like South Africa, is power sharing a better basis for democracy than outright majority rule?

   1 Yes   2 Uncertain   3 No

3. During the transitional period following the first non-racial elections in South Africa, is power sharing necessary for reconciliation?

   1 Yes   2 Have reservations   3 No

4. During the same transitional period, is power sharing necessary for peace?

   1. Yes   2 Have reservations   3 No

5. During the same transitional period, is power sharing necessary for stability?

   1 Yes   2 Have reservations   3 No

6. Should power sharing in South Africa be limited to a period of five years i.e. the duration of the transitional government of national unity?

1 Yes   2 Have reservations   3 No

7. Should power sharing arrangements be extended beyond the limited period of five years?

1 Yes   2 Have reservations   3 No

8. Should power sharing be a permanent feature of the South African political structure?

1 Yes   2 Have reservations   3 No

9. The period leading to the first non-racial elections was marked by widespread violence and political intimidation in some parts of the country. In light of that widespread violence and political intimidation, to what extent were you apprehensive about the political future of the new South Africa?

1 Very much   2 To an appreciable extent   3 To some extent
4 Not at all

10. Do you think that power sharing contributed to the reduction of political violence after the elections?

1 Yes   2 Uncertain   3 No

11. The concept of power sharing is central to this study. In the space provided below, feel free to elaborate further on its advantages and/or disadvantages:

225

Political Parties

12. The following are some of the groups that participated in the 1994 non-racial national elections. For which party did you vote? Choose one:

1. African National Congress (ANC)
2. National Party (NP)
3. Inkatha Freedom Party (IFP)
4. Freedom Front (FF)
5. Democratic Party (DM)
6. Pan Africans Congress (PAC)
7. Others
8. Did not vote

13. In South Africa, where the two major racial sections of the population are black and white, political choices can be influenced by racial preferences. Did race play any part in the choice of your group?

1 Definitely Yes   2 Yes   3 No   4 Definitely No

14. In South Africa, where there are many ethnic groups (e.g. English, Afrikaner, Zulu, Xhosa, Sotho etc.) political choices can be influenced by ethnic preferences. Did ethnicity play any part in the choice of your group?

1 Definitely Yes   2 Yes   3 No   4 Definitely No

15. Were you or were you not satisfied with the results of the first non-racial elections in South Africa?

    1 Not satisfied   2 Slightly satisfied

    3 Moderately satisfied   4 Very satisfied

16. For which party would you vote if elections were held today? Choose one

    1. African National Congress (ANC)
    2. National Party (NP)
    3. Inkatha Freedom Party (IFP)
    4. Freedom Front (FF)
    5. Democratic Party (DP)
    6. Pan Africanist Congress (PAC)
    7. Others
    8. Would not vote

17. Do you agree or disagree that the first non-racial election in the history of South Africa was really about getting rid of apartheid?

    1 Agree   2 Uncertain   3 Disagree

18. Do you agree or disagree with the statement that the test of the new democracy in South Africa is not the first election but subsequent ones?

    1 Agree   2 Uncertain   3 Disagree

Equality

19. If racial equality is defined as equal treatment of all racial groups under the law, to what extent are you in favor or against racial equality?

    1 Definitely in favor   2 In favor
    3 Against   4 Definitely against

20. Do you think that in the new South Africa blacks now receive equal treatment under the law?

    1 Yes   2 Uncertain   3 No

21. Do you think that racial equality will be realized in South Africa?

    1 Yes   2 Possibly   3 Doubtful   4 No

22. How long do you think it might take South Africa to realize racial equality? Choose one:

    1 Years   2 Decades   3 A century   4   Two   or   more
    centuries   5 Never

Ethnicity

23. People all over the world come from a variety of backgrounds, cultures, ethnic and/or racial groups. There are many different words to name these groups. Some examples of such groups are African Americans, the Irish, Spaniards, Africans, Europeans, West Indians, Scots, whites and blacks. Most people regard a specific ethnic, cultural or racial group as their own and will describe themselves in terms of their membership of that group. A person will, for example, say: "I am Matebele" or "I am a Scot."

Please tell who you are in terms of your membership of an ethnic, cultural or racial group. Begin your answer with

I am a _____

24. With which one of the following groups do you identify the **most**?

Please note that you can choose only **one** group. **NOTE: PLEASE READ THROUGH THE WHOLE LIST OF ALTERNATIVESBEFORE MAKING A CHOICE.**

None/Do not identify with any group	01
Do not know	02
Africans	03
South Africans	04
Blacks	05
Whites/Europeans	06
Afrikaners/Afrikaans-speaking whites	07
Afrikaans people (all people with Afrikaans as home language - including coloureds)	08
English-speaking whites	09
Coloureds	10
Indians	11
Zulus	12
Swazis	13
Xhosas	14
Southern Sothos	15
Northern Sothos or Pedis	16
Tswanas or Western Sothos	17
Shangaans/Tsongas	18
Vendas/Lembas	19
Other European/white or Asian groups (e.g. Greeks, Portuguese, Americans, Germans, Chinese etc.)	20
Other	21

25. To what degree do you identify with **each** of the following groups?

	To a large degree	To a reasonable degree	To a small degree	Not at all
Africans	1	2	3	4
South Africans	1	2	3	4
Blacks	1	2	3	4
Whites	1	2	3	4
Afrikaners/Afrikaans-speaking whites	1	2	3	4
Afrikaans people (all people speaking Afrikaans - including Coloureds)	1	2	3	4
English-speaking whites	1	2	3	4
Coloureds	1	2	3	4
Indians	1	2	3	4
Other European/white or Asian groups (e.g. Greeks, Portuguese, Americans, Chinese etc.)	1	2	3	4
A specific black ethnic group (e.g. Zulus, Xhosas, Northern Sothos or Pedis, Tswanas etc.	1	2	3	4

26. The following statements may indicate how you feel about your ethnic or cultural group. Please indicate whether you *agree strongly* (1), *agree* (2), *are neutral* (3) *disagree* (4), *disagree strongly* (5) with each statement.

	Strongly agree	Agree to some extent	Neutral	Disagree to some extent	Strongly disagree
Loyalty towards my own ethnic or cultural group is important to me	1	2	3	4	5
Commitment to the culture of my own ethnic or cultural group is a major source of security in my life	1	2	3	4	5
I will take action if the identity of my ethnic or cultural group is threatened	1	2	3	4	5
It upsets me when other people speak negatively about my own ethnic or cultural group	1	2	3	4	5
I do not want to belong to any other ethnic or cultural group	1	2	3	4	5
I respect a person who takes pride in the special qualities of his or her own ethnic or cultural group	1	2	3	4	5
I am happy that I am a member of the ethnic or cultural group that I belong to	1	2	3	4	5
I have a lot of pride in my ethnic or cultural group and its accomplishments	1	2	3	4	5
I have a strong sense of belonging to my own ethnic or cultural group	1	2	3	4	5
I feel a strong attachment towards my own ethnic or cultural group	1	2	3	4	5

27. Please indicate to what extent you agree or disagree with the following statements:

	Strongly agree	Agree	Neutral	Disagree	Strongly disagree
Members of my ethnic or cultural group should mobilize to protect their identity and interests	1	2	3	4	5
The rights of minority groups should be protected in the new South Africa	1	2	3	4	5
My ethnic or cultural group should enjoy self-determination and autonomy within a new South Africa	1	2	3	4	5
The constitution renders sufficient protection for the language and culture of my own ethnic or cultural group	1	2	3	4	5
The identity and/or culture of my ethnic or cultural group is threatened	1	2	3	4	5

28. If all ethnic groups are accorded equal status under the law, then ethnic groups can be said to have ethnic equality. To what extent are you in favor or against ethnic equality?

    1 Definitely in favor   2 In favor

    3 Against   4 Definitely against

29. Do you think that ethnic equality will be realized in South Africa?

    1 Yes   2 Possibly   3 Doubtful   4 No

30. How long do you think it might take South Africa to realize ethnic equality? Choose **one**:

    1 Years   2 Decades   3 A century 4 Two or more centuries

    5 Never

Democracy

31. In a representative multiparty democracy, the adult population has a right to vote with a choice between political parties. To what extent are you in favor or against such a type of democracy?

    1 Strongly in favor   2 In favor

    3 Against   4 Strongly against

32. In a representative one-party system, the adult population has a right to vote for individual candidates within the same party. To what extent are you in favor or against such a political system?

1 Definitely in favor   2 In favor

3 Against   4 Strongly against

33. Are you for or against majority rule?

1 For   2 Have reservations   3 Against

34. Do you believe that absolute black majority rule is inevitable in South Africa?

1 Yes   2 Uncertain   3 No

35. Do you believe that in South Africa, black majority rule will amount to Black domination?

1 Yes   2 Uncertain   3 No

36. Do you believe that black majority rule in South Africa will cause white alienation?

1 Yes   2 Possibly   3 Doubtful   4 No

37. Do you believe that black majority rule will result in racial conflict?

1 Yes   2 Possibly   3 Doubtful   4 No

38. Among the major political systems proposed for South Africa are: (1) A unitary structure in which political power is centralized, (2) A federal structure in which power is decentralized and devolves to the nine provinces and (3) A consociational structure in which executive power is shared by the elites of various racial and ethnic groups (e.g. English, Afrikaners, Coloureds, Indians, Zulus, Sothos etc.) that have communal autonomy and can exercise mutual vetoes to protect their interests. Which of the following political systems would you prefer for South Africa? Choose **one**:

1 Unitary system

2 Federal system

3 Consociational system

39. Which political system, as stated above, would be ideal for racial harmony in South Africa?

1	2	3	4 None

40. Which political system would be ideal for ethnic harmony in South Africa?

1	2	3	4 None

41. Which political system would be ideal for democracy in South Africa?

1	2	3	4 None

42. Which political system, if any, should be entrenched in a new South African constitution?

1   2   3   4 None

At this point I would like to shift to related issues that may have a major impact on power-sharing, racial equality and democracy in South Africa.

The economy

43. Do you agree or disagree with the statement that, because of the legacy of apartheid, the majority of whites in South Africa have greater economic power than blacks?

1 Agree   2 Uncertain   3 Disagree

44. How would you categorize the present socio-economic gap between whites and blacks in South Africa?

1 Very large   2 Large   3 Medium   4 Small   5 Very small

45. What are your expectations about the socio-economic gap between whites and blacks in South Africa five years from now?

1 Very large   2 Large   3 Medium   4 Small   5 Very small

46. Do you agree or disagree with the statement that political power sharing does not necessarily mean economic power sharing?

1 Agree   2 Uncertain   3 Disagree

47. Are you in favor or against the distribution of wealth through higher taxes for the rich?

1 Definitely in favor   2 In favor
3 Against   4 Definitely against

48. Do you agree or disagree with the statement that the current state of economic inequality in South Africa has the potential for racial conflict?

1 Agree   2 Uncertain   3 Disagree

49. The current government of national unity (GNU) has put considerable faith in the business sector as the main engine for economic growth and development. Are you in favor or against that policy?

1 In Favor   2 Have reservations   3 Against

50. Do you agree or disagree with the statement that the current state of economic inequality in South Africa has a potential for class conflict?

1 Agree   2 Uncertain   3 Disagree

51. Do you think the Reconstruction and Development Program (RDP) of the current government will effectively narrow the gap between the rich and poor in South Africa?

1 Yes   2 Possible   3 Doubtful   4 No

52. Do you think that the Western-style market economy will succeed in narrowing the gap between the rich and poor in South Africa?

1 Yes   2 Possible   3 Doubtful   4 No

53. Do you think that socialism could be a better system than capitalism in narrowing the gap between the rich and the poor in South Africa?

1 Yes   2 Possible   3 Doubtful   4 No

54. Do you think that the government should resort to nationalization of the commanding heights of the economy to narrow the gap between the rich and the poor in South Africa?

1 Yes   2 Uncertain   3 No

55. If the government does not succeed in narrowing the gap between the rich and the poor through the RDP, do you think the new South Africa may be headed for a major conflict?

1 Yes   2 Possible   3 Doubtful   4 No

56. Do you think the crime rate would soar if the gap between the rich and the poor is not reduced?

1 Yes   2 Possible   3 Doubtful   4 No

57. The new South Africa is experiencing a period of relative peace and goodwill. Do you think that the climate of peace and goodwill will continue, if the GNU is not successful in upgrading the socioeconomic conditions of Black people?

1 Yes   2 Uncertain   3 No

Workers

58. The government of national unity has called upon black workers to tighten their belts in the interest of economic growth and development. Are you for or against that specific policy?

1 For   2 Uncertain   3 Against

59. Do you think that workers should be denied more wages in order to maintain higher productivity?

1 Yes   2 Uncertain   3 No

60. Do you think that black workers in South Africa will wait for economic growth and development before pressing their demands for better wages through strike action?

1 Yes   2 Possible   3 Doubtful   4 No

240

61. Do you think that, if there is successful growth and development, employers will voluntarily give workers better wages?

1 Yes   2 Possible   3 Doubtful   4 No

62. Are you in favor or against the use of strike action by workers?

1 Yes   2 Have reservations   3 No

63. Do you think employers should have the constitutional right to lock out striking workers?

1 Yes   2 Uncertain   3 No

Affirmative Action

64. The GNU is using affirmative action to enable blacks to have better opportunities for employment. Are you in favor or against affirmative action?

1 Strongly in favor   2 in favor

3 Against   4 Strongly against

65. Do you think affirmative action will serve to portray blacks as unqualified workers in the eyes of white workers?

1 Yes   2 Uncertain   3 No

66. Do you think that white workers would be justified in viewing affirmative action as reverse discrimination?

1 Yes   2 Uncertain   3 No

67. Do you think that affirmative action will contribute to bad race relations in South Africa?

1 Yes   2 Uncertain   3 No

Education

68. Do you agree or disagree that the educational system in South Africa needs radical transformation to enable blacks to get good education?

1 Strongly agree   2 Agree
3 Disagree   4 Strongly disagree

69. How would you rate the standard of education in black schools?

1 Excellent   2 Good   3 Fair   4 Poor 5 Very poor

70. How would you rate the standard of education in white schools?

1 Excellent   2 Good   3 Fair   4 Poor 5 Very poor

242

71. How would you rate the standard of education in traditionally segregated black universities?

1 Excellent 2 Good 3 Fair 4 Poor 5 Very poor

72. How would you rate the standard of education in traditionally white universities?

1 Excellent 2 Good 3 Fair 4 Poor 5 Very poor

73. The following is a list of South African universities. In terms of educational productivity and prestige, which ones would you rank as the top five?: Circle five numbers only

1 Cape Town	11 Pretoria
2 Boputhatswana	12 Rand Afrikaans
3 Durban-Westville	13 Rhodes
4 Fort Hare	14 South Africa
5 Medunsa	15 Stellenbosch
6 Natal	16 Transkei
7 North	17 Western Cape
8 Orange Free State	18 Witwatersrand
9 Port Elizabeth	19 Zululand
10 Potchefstroom	20 Vista

74. In terms of educational productivity and prestige, which of the above listed universities would you rank as the bottom five? write down five numbers only

Language

75. South Africa is the only country in the world with eleven official languages. Are you in favor or against the existence of so many official languages?

    1 Strongly in favor   2 In favor   3 Uncertain

    4 Against   5 Strongly against

76. Do you agree or disagree with the statement that the national interests of the country would be better served by one official language?

    1 Strongly agree   2 Agree   3 Disagree   4 Strongly disagree

77. Are you for or against English as the only official language?

    1 Definitely For   2 For   3 Against   4 Definitely against

78. If English was made the only official language in South Africa, do you think that your language would in effect be demoted?

    1 Definitely Yes   2 Yes   3 No   4 Definitely against

79. Are you for or against the holding of a national referendum to decide on the question of English as the only official language in South Africa?

    1 Definitely For   2 For   3 Against   4 Definitely against

80. If the majority of South Africans participating in the proposed referendum endorse English as the only official language, would you accept or reject that national decision?

1 Definitely accept   2 Accept   3 Reject   4 Definitely reject

81. Language is the main vehicle of a culture. To what extent do you support the right of different racial and ethnic groups to preserve and maintain their own languages?

1 Very much   2 To an appreciable extent
3 To some extent   4 Not at all

National anthem

82. The new South Africa has two national anthems i.e. NKOSI SIKELEL 'IAFRIKA/MORENA BOLOKA SECHABA SA HESO and DIE STEM. To what extent are you in favor or against the existence of two national anthems in South Africa?

1 Strongly in favor   2 Moderately in favor
3 Moderately against   4 Strongly against

83. To what extent would you be in favor or against one amalgamated national anthem which combines parts from NKOSI SIKELEL 'IAFRIKA/MORENA BOLOKA SECHABA SA HESO and DIE STEM?

1 Strongly in favor   2 Moderately in favor
3 Moderately against   4 Strongly against

Leaders

84. Do you agree or disagree that F.W. de Klerk played a major role in persuading the white electorate to abandon apartheid?

    1 Agree   2 Uncertain   3 Disagree

85. Do you agree or disagree that F.W. de Klerk played a major role in persuading the white electorate to accept change?

    1 Agree   2 Uncertain   3 Disagree

86. Do you agree or disagree that Nelson Mandela has made a major contribution to the struggle for freedom in South Africa?

    1 Agree   2 Uncertain   3 Disagree

87. Do you agree or disagree that Nelson Mandela has done much, since his inauguration as president, to restore confidence in democracy in the new South Africa?

    1 Agree   2 Uncertain   3 Disagree

88. Do you agree that president Nelson Mandela is currently the social glue that keeps blacks and whites together?

    1 Agree   2 Have reservations   3 Disagree

89. To what extent are you apprehensive about the future stability of South Africa after Mandela?

    1 Not apprehensive at all   2 Slightly apprehensive
    3 Moderately apprehensive   4 Very much apprehensive

Finally, I would like to obtain some information relating to your background:

90. Age (recorded in digits)

91. Gender
    1 Female____   2 Male____

92. Personal status
    1 Single_____   2 Married_____   3 Widowed_____   4 Divorced___

93. Number of children
    1 None_____   2 One_____   3 Two_____4 Three_____
    5 Four or more_____

94. Education
    Which type of schools did you attend at the primary level?

    1 Private (whites only)_____   2 Private (multiracial)_____
    3 Public (whites only)_____   4 Public (blacks only)_____

95. Which type of schools did you attend at the secondary level?

    1 Private (whites only)_____   2 Private (multiracial)_____

    3 Public (whites only)_____   4 Public (blacks only)_____

96. What is your major (or majors, if applicable) at the university you are currently attending?

_____

97. Religion:

    What is your religion, if any?

    1 Catholic____   2 Protestant_____   3 Jewish_____   4 Moslem___

    5 Other_____

    If other please write in name:_____

98. Class

    How would you define your social class standing?

    1 Upper class_____   2 Middle class_____3 Working class_____

    4 Under class_____

99. Place of residence:

    Where is your home located?

    1 Integrated urban area_____   2 Non integrated urban area_____

    3 Rural area_____

100. What is the name of the university you are currently attending?

Name:_____

THANK YOU FOR YOUR COOPERATION

Index

AFRICAN STUDIES

35. Toyin Falola, A. Ajayi, A. Alao, B. Babawale, **The Military Factor in Nigeria 1966-1985**

36. Samba Diop, **The Oral History and Literature of the Wolof People of Waalo, Northern Senegal: The Master of the Word (Griot) in the Wolof Tradition**

37. Rina Okonkwo, **Protest Movements in Lagos, 1908-1930**

38. Felton Best (editor), **Black Resistance Movements in the United States and Africa, 1800-1993**

39. Jeffrey C. Stone, **A Short History of the Cartography of Africa**

40. H.L. Pretorius, **Historiography and Historical Sources Regarding African Indigenous Churches in South Africa**

41. Michael Okema, **Political Culture of Tanzania**

42. Alven Makapela, **The Problem with Africanity in the Seventh-Day Adventist Church**

43. Patrick E. Idoye, **Theatre and Social Change in Zambia: The Chikwakwa Theatre**

44. M.C. Kitshoff (ed.), **African Independent Churches Today: Kaleidoscope of Afro-Christianity**

45. Charles O. Chikeka, **Decolonization Process in Africa During the Post-War Era, 1960-1990**

46. Santosh C. Saha, **Culture in Liberia: An Afrocentric View of the Cultural Interaction Between the Indigenous Liberians and the Americo-Liberians**

47. John Mukum Mbaku (ed.), **Corruption and the Crisis of Institutional Reforms in Africa**

48. Immaculate N. Kizza, **Africa's Indigenous Institutions in Nation Building: Uganda**

49. Tayo Oke, **Radicalism, Political Power and Foreign Policy in Nigeria**

50. Wayne Madsen, **Genocide and Covert Operations in Africa, 1993-1999**

51. Jim Ocitti, **Political Evolution and Democratic Practice in Uganda 1952-1996**

52. Gary Y. Okihiro, **A Social History of the Bakwena and Peoples of the Kalahari of Southern Africa, 19th Century**

53. Ritchard Tamba M'Bayo, Chuka Onwumechili, R. Nwafo Nwanko (eds.), **Press and Politics in Africa**